The *Friendship Book*

of Francis Gay

A THOUGHT
FOR EACH DAY
IN 2008

D. C. THOMSON & CO., LTD.
London Glasgow Manchester Dundee

A book is like a garden carried in a pocket.
Chinese Proverb.

January

AT the start of another New Year I'm reminded of "The Gate Of The Year" by Minnie Louise Hoskins. King George VI quoted it in his Christmas message to the nation and it's still as reassuringly valid today.

"I said to the man who stood at the gate of the year, 'Give me light that I may tread safely into the unknown.' And he replied, 'Go out into the darkness and put your hand in the hand of God. That shall be to you better than light and safer than a known way.'"

THE planting of a garden
  The making of a home,
The whisper of a quiet prayer
  When we are on our own.
The soothing of a fretful child
  And hands that calm and bless,
The light on happy faces
  Which smile in tenderness.
It's in the simple things of life
  An inner joy we find,
Refreshment for the spirit
  Contentment for the mind.

            Kathleen Gillum.

Thursday — **January 3**

WE always receive a long letter from our friend John in the United States soon after New Year. On one occasion he wrote:

"Life is sweet and precious, a great gift to be appreciated. Love and friendship enhance life and, as the years have gone by, I have come to know the truth of these words by Aristotle: 'Friendship is a slow-ripening fruit.'

"In this New Year I wish you hours touched by sunshine and few shadows, in the words of Winston Churchill, 'a wise and kindly way of life'."

And the Lady of the House and I, in turn, wish you the very same!

Friday — **January 4**

FIONA will never forget her grandmother. "She had the loveliest laugh," she recalled. "It was like a church bell tinkling out merrily, inviting all her friends and family to share her zest for life."

This recollection reminded me of the saying: "Laugh and the world laughs with you." The sound of laughter echoing across a room can indeed be infectious.

Descriptions of laughter include the evocative "God's sunshine" and the happy times in life are what most of us prefer to keep in mind.

Fun and light-hearted moments should be prescribed as a recommended part of daily living, to be taken at least once daily, preferably with friends.

Saturday — *January 5*

IT has to be said, January isn't everybody's favourite month. After the busy sociable sparkle of December and the flurry of the New Year, the grey days of January can bring distinct feelings of anti-climax, particularly if we allow ourselves to brood about the long wait until Spring arrives.

However, I for one am not going to be too quick to put away my copy of Charles Dickens' "A Christmas Carol" on the shelf. Instead, I shall do my best to keep the example of the reformed Scrooge, who vowed, "I will honour Christmas in my heart, and try to keep it all the year."

If we can do that, what a wonderful twelve months it will be!

Sunday — *January 6*

BUT the men marvelled, saying, What manner of man is this, that even the winds and the sea obey him!   Matthew 8:27

Monday — *January 7*

LOUISE loves her job as a primary school teacher and her pupils obviously like and respect her. I had heard from some of the mothers how she brings out the best in their children.

When I met her I asked her how she did it. What was the secret?

"It's no secret," she laughed. "I praise them! That's often all they need. A little praise can turn a loser into a winner."

It's worth remembering, isn't it?

Tuesday — **January 8**

READING a biography of Johnny Cash our friend Chris was delighted to discover that one of the singer's favourite inspirational verses was also one of his. Written by an anonymous author, it had been copied down in the 1940s and Mr Cash had kept it thereafter. It read:

When I am dead if men can say,
"He helped the world upon its way,"
If they can say, if they but can,
"He did his best. He played the man,
His way was straight, his soul was clean,
His life was not unkind or mean.
He always did his best and tried
To help men," — I'll be satisfied.

Of course he didn't always live that kind of life but then these words weren't written for saints. They were written for folk like us all who may fail but still aspire to better things and hope to go home in the end with our heads held high — just like Mr Cash.

Wednesday — **January 9**

IT was just a sheet of paper stuck in a shop window, inviting people along to an evening meeting at a church hall. It promised good company and stories of how faith had turned lives around. It ended by saying:

Everyone Welcome
Refreshment Will Be Provided
Admission Free (Someone Else Already
Paid For You)

Well, put like that, how could anyone refuse?

Thursday — **January 10**

PEACEFUL PLACE

SOMEWHERE, just along the road
We'll find a peaceful place,
Beyond the troubles of the world
    A quiet, breathing space.
A place where sunlight warms the air
    And gentle breezes blow,
Where we'll discover joy once more
    And dreams of long ago.

Somewhere, just along the road —
    It can't be very far,
We'll leave the problems of the day
    And seek the evening star.
A quiet place, a breathing space
    It waits for you and I.
And somewhere, just along the road
    We'll find it, by and by.

Iris Hesselden.

Friday — **January 11**

WHEN we say goodbye to someone we are using a shortened version of the old expression "God be with you".

It's a pity that "farewell", as a parting wish, is not often heard now. It means, literally, "May you fare well".

The Scottish version, "Fare ye weel", has a fine ring to it and I also like another expression still in use in Scotland, "Haste ye back" — hurry back.

No-one likes parting with friends or relatives but it helps if we can leave them with a sincere and heartfelt wish.

FROSTY FRAME

Saturday — *January 12*

JAMES had always been an academic high-flyer, and on leaving university quickly found himself a well-paid job in finance. However, it wasn't long before he discovered that a demanding career brings its own stresses, and he was sometimes turned into a person that he didn't want to be.

Happily, James had the courage to make changes to his values and outlook. Now he keeps a copy of this rhyme as a little reminder:

If you often lose your patience with the
*   people that you meet,*
If you walk the world in anger, in frustration
*   and defeat,*
Then turn around, and make a vow to open
*   up your mind,*
And soon, in fellow humans, you will very
*   quickly find*
There's much to love in others, if you open
*   up the door,*
And better still — you'll realise you like
*   yourself much more!*

Sunday — *January 13*

NOW therefore, I pray thee, pardon my sin, and turn again with me, that I may worship the Lord.   Samuel I 15:25

Monday — *January 14*

FED up of another wet and dreary Winter's day? Well, this Arabic saying will surely put your thoughts into perspective.

All sunshine makes the desert.

Tuesday — *January 15*

WHEN Mike went off to walk the North Devon Coastal Path, I was bemused to receive a postcard which showed a glorious view of cliffs and sea, but which bore only the message: "This trip is just like life."

On his return he gave me the explanation. "The journey was certainly full of interest," he told me, "But, oh — it was equally full of ups and downs. Yet every time I managed to successfully slog my way up a hill, I was rewarded by the most glorious vistas — and by the satisfaction of being able to look back to see just how far I'd come."

I think Mike's message was right. And I'll keep that postcard to remind me that there are wonderful views which await those who don't give up!

Wednesday — *January 16*

WORRIES — we all have them. But perhaps we sometimes have a tendency to worry for no good reason.

I like the story of the millionaire businessman and film producer, J. Arthur Rank. Having little time to waste he decided that he would do all of his worrying on the one day — Wednesday.

Each time a worry loomed Mr Rank would write it down on a piece of paper, fold it, slip it into a wooden box and forget about it until the following Wednesday. The amazing thing was that when he opened the box again most of the things he might have spent time fretting over had already taken care of themselves.

Thursday — **January 17**

THE Lady of the House read this advice given by a mother to a child, and overheard by the American writer Oliver Wendell Holmes.

"Take your needle, my child, and work at your pattern; it will come out a rose by and by."

Life's like that; one stitch at a time, taken patiently, will ensure that the pattern will work out all right in the end.

Friday — **January 18**

MOST of us have a few long-standing friends we somehow see very little of. However, that doesn't make them any less effective as friends. A real friend might live on the other side of the world; you might not have shaken their hand for more years than you care to remember, but just knowing they are thinking of you can mean a lot.

These words, quoted by our friend Grant, warmed my heart.

Make a wish, then close your eyes,
Forget all the lows, just go for the highs.
Dance to the moon, yes, climb to the top,
Dance to the stars, with a spring and a hop.
But if that star fades and you think it has gone,
I'll always be there — to switch it back on.

Saturday — **January 19**

HOLDING on to anger is like grasping a hot coal with the intent of throwing it at someone else; you are the one who gets burned.

Buddha.

Sunday — *January 20*

THOU, O Lord, remainest for ever; thy throne from generation to generation.

Lamentations 5:19

Monday — *January 21*

ERIC is a youth worker, and it's a vocation which has brought him into contact with many troubled young people. "It can often be frustrating," he admitted, "but whenever I feel tempted to give up on someone I remind myself of the words of the American minister, Robert H. Schuller, who said, 'Anyone can count the seeds in an apple, but only God can count the number of apples in a seed.'

"In other words," Eric continued, "We must always be prepared to see beyond the obvious facts. An apple pip may look very small and unpromising but just like people, when they're given the right encouragement to grow, they can produce no end of good things."

And that's certainly not just pie in the sky!

Tuesday — *January 22*

DURING a recital seventeen-year-old Alan played a trumpet solo. All went well until he made a mistake in the third verse.

Later he lamented that his one wrong note had ruined the song. His mother replied, "That's not true at all! It's the five hundred and twenty-eight perfect notes you played which everyone will remember."

What a positive way to look at life!

Wednesday — **January 23**

DENISE had been going through a difficult time. Her spirits were raised, however, by the gift of flowers from an old schoolfriend. Though the blooms themselves were welcome, it was the attached card which really brought comfort, with these words by Sydney Bremer:

"Hope is the companion of power and the mother of success, for those of us who hope strongest have within us the gift of miracles."

Cheering words to bring light into darkness.

Thursday — **January 24**

THE name Susan Coolidge might not be instantly recognisable but anyone who knows "What Katy Did" and "What Katy Did Next" will recognise her as one of the more popular authors of the 19th century. She isn't so well known for her poetry but this verse is memorable:

Every day is a fresh beginning,
Listen my soul to the glad refrain.
And, in spite of old sorrows
And older sinning,
Troubles forecasted
And possible pain,
Take heart with the day
And begin again.

Friday — **January 25**

I READ this thought in a favourite magazine:
Isn't it strange how a teapot can represent at the same time the comforts of solitude and the pleasures of company?

Saturday — **January 26**

*H*ONOUR is the field I chose
    To build my house upon
Winds of truth and virtue blow
    Across the verdant lawn.
Courage is the tree I grew
    Beside my hedgerows tall,
Its shade imparts assurance to
    My spirits when they fall.
Wisdom is the garden bright
    I planted by the well.
And where I gather blooms of light
    No darkness can dispel.

                    Rachel Wallace-Oberle.

Sunday — **January 27**

*C*OMMIT thy works unto the Lord, and thy
    thoughts shall be established.   Proverbs 16:3

Monday — **January 28**

*W*HEN Ian was young there were three words
    he was warned never to use: *I don't care.*

The person who warned him explained why.
"You will start by saying 'I don't care' about little
things — a message you forgot to pass on, a letter
you ought to have written, a plate you broke.

"Before you know it you will be saying you don't
care about things that really matter. You will let
your friends down, you will make mistakes and not
bother to put them right.

"Never say 'I don't care'. Say you do care — and
mean it."

Tuesday — **January 29**

How delightful it is to step out in the morning and hear the birds singing. Ornithologists will tell you that birds sing to attract a mate, but there's another explanation which is much closer to my heart.

An ancient Jewish legend has it that after creating the world and before creating Man, God took a break. He gathered the angels around and asked what they thought of His work so far. All agreed the Earth was a masterpiece.

Then one angel dared to suggest it lacked a little something. No one could figure out what he meant until he said the world lacked only the sound of praise for its Creator.

And so God created birdsong.

Wednesday — **January 30**

We have all heard the expression "Pride comes before a fall". Here are two more on pride to consider:

Pride is like a man's beard. It just keeps growing and has to be shaved every day.

God sends no-one away empty except those who are already too full of themselves.

Humbling, isn't it?

Thursday — **January 31**

One of the most inspiring quotes I've ever heard was uttered by St Francis of Assisi who said, "Preach the gospel always and when necessary use words."

That's what I call thought-provoking.

HIGHLAND
WINTER

February

A SINGLE moment of understanding can flood a whole life with meaning.

THE Lady of the House and I were enjoying a visit to our friends Jim and Margaret. After lunch they promised us a treat, and led us through a snow-dusted garden iced with frost to where a small carpet of snowdrops was flowering beneath Winter jasmine and a red-berried hedge, the whole scene lit by a low sun. It was a sight to lift the heart.

Snowdrops are much loved "milk flowers", bridging the gap between seasons. They are associated with both the Virgin Mary and Eve.

Legend says that when Adam and Eve were banished from the Garden of Eden, Eve cried tears of repentance in the wilderness. An angel, seeing them fall to the barren ground, pitied her and turned them into snowdrops.

Candlemas Day, 2nd February, has long honoured the Virgin Mary. Candles are lit and snowdrops, the "Fair Maids Of February", symbolic of purity, decorate churches. This explains these old names for snowdrops — Mary's Tapers and Candlemas Bells.

Sunday — *February 3*

SO will I sing praise unto thy name for ever, that I may daily perform my vows. Psalms 61:8

Monday — *February 4*

A DAY is too precious to let it pass by unnoticed. Each evening I like to set aside a minute or two just to take stock. Have I been the friend I should have been today? Do I need to try harder tomorrow? George Eliot put it this way:

If you sit down at set of sun
And count the acts that you have done,
And, counting, find
One self-denying deed, one word
That eased the heart of him who heard,
One glance most kind
That fell like sunshine where it went —
Then you may count that day well spent.

Tuesday — *February 5*

I WAS talking to a wise neighbour about the use of money. "Do you consider it to be the root of all evil?" I asked him.

"It seems to me," he said after some consideration, "that if only we could regard money as something to be shared, it would become our servant for good.

"If, however, we regard it as something to be hoarded, it becomes our master. If, on the other hand, we regard it as something to be used with love, it becomes one of the world's great powers."

Wednesday — *February 6*

FROM time to time I dip into my well-thumbed scrapbook and I always come across something I want to pass on. I hope you like these lines:

We live in little minutes,
Time comes not in a mass,
So keep a smile, it's well worth while,
Whatever comes to pass.

Thursday — *February 7*

NO-ONE would have been surprised if Nelson Mandela had emerged from his years of captivity a bitter man, but instead he turned inward, examining his soul, and finding moral courage and insight. It is from him that we receive these words of encouragement:

"Our worst fear is not that we are inadequate. Our deepest fear is that we are powerful beyond measure. It is our light, not our darkness that most frightens us. We ask ourselves, 'Who am I to be brilliant, gorgeous, talented and fabulous?' Actually, who are you *not* to be?

"You are a child of God: your playing small doesn't serve the world. There is nothing enlightened about shrinking so that other people won't feel insecure around you.

"We were born to make manifest the glory of God within us. It is not just in some of us, it is in everyone, and as we let our own light shine, we unconsciously give other people permission to do the same. As we are liberated from our own fear, our presence automatically liberates others."

Friday — **February 8**

RAMBLING wasn't a pastime in Jack's younger days. It was simply the best way to get from farm to farm when he was looking for work.

"Sometimes I'd find my path blocked by a stream that looked as if it might give me some trouble," he recalled. "So, the first thing I'd do was to take off my jacket and throw it across to the other side. Then I'd set about joining it."

How often, I wondered, are we put off from doing something we know we really should by the thought of the difficulties we might meet on the way? Why not follow Jack's example? Let's make our best intentions like his jacket, throw them over our troubles and follow after them.

Saturday — **February 9**

BOOKS have always been a passion of mine, so I was interested to read what others have thought of the bound page.

John Milton, the author of "Paradise Lost", described a good book as "the precious life-blood of a master spirit, embalmed and treasured up on purpose to a life beyond life".

To Martin Tupper it meant, "the best of friends, the same today and for ever". Then John Ruskin thought that there were only two kinds of book: "the books of the hour and the books of all time".

Sunday — **February 10**

TAKE therefore no thought for the morrow: for the morrow shall take thought for the things of itself.
                                                    Matthew 6:34

Monday — *February 11*

IMAGINE being deaf, dumb — and blind. Helen Keller was born with all of these difficulties to face, but as an adult she toured America raising funds for the American Foundation For The Blind and campaigning for people with disabilities like hers who were often housed in asylums.

This inspirational woman came into this life faced with seemingly insurmountable problems, but she left it having discovered a great secret. "Life is an exciting business," she said. "And it is most exciting when it is lived for others."

Tuesday — *February 12*

THE gift of the morning,
The peace of the evening,
The strength of the mountains,
*   The calm of the dales.*
The wind from the ocean.
*   The tang of salt breezes,*
The tide ever flowing,
*   The sight of white sails.*

The thrill of exploring,
*   New things to discover,*
New people, new places,
*   Whenever we roam.*
The joy of returning,
*   One bright star to lead us,*
The shelter and comfort,
*   The blessings of home.*
                              Iris Hesselden.

PURE
PERFECTION

Wednesday — **February 13**

WE witnessed a spectacular rainstorm early one evening, and then, an hour later, the clouds broke to reveal a beautiful rainbow.

The transition from the frightening moments of thunder and rain to the colourful beauty of the storm's peaceful aftermath was surely rather like life itself. There is nearly always a welcome respite from fear and worry when you have gone through a trauma or a crisis, and emerged stronger.

As Lord Byron wrote: "The evening beam that smiles the clouds away and tints tomorrow with prophetic ray."

Thursday — **February 14**

THOSE of us who receive a Valentine card today might like to know there really was a St Valentine and he really did die for love — the love of God. And he seems to have been quite the romantic as well.

A Roman priest, Valentine helped the early persecuted Christians and eventually became one. Engaged couples who wanted Christian marriages had to exchange vows in secret. Priests carrying out these ceremonies risked death, but it was a risk Valentine thought worth taking.

Eventually, he was caught and, while waiting for execution, legend has it he restored the sight of his jailer's daughter. She fell in love with him and pleaded for his life, but to no avail. The night before he died Valentine wrote to her, signing his note, "From your Valentine".

Loving messages have been exchanged in Valentine's name ever since.

Friday — **February 15**

EMILY Dickinson, the American poet, wrote these delightful lines:

If I can stop one heart from breaking,
I shall not live in vain;
If I can ease one life the aching,
Or cool one pain,
Or help one fainting robin
Unto his nest again,
I shall not live in vain.

Saturday — **February 16**

AN old shepherd told me he once had a lamb that had strayed too close to a cliff edge and fell several feet on to a ledge below.

When he discovered what had happened, the farmer lowered the shepherd by a rope to try to retrieve the creature. However, the nearer he approached, the more distressed the lamb appeared. There was a danger that, if he was any closer, the young creature might fall off the ledge.

After a good deal of head scratching, the shepherd tied the lamb's mother to a cradle of rope and lowered her instead. Reassured, the lamb calmed down straightaway. The shepherd was able to scramble down, lift his lamb to safety and then recover the sheep.

A tale which reflects the power of a mother's devotion.

Sunday — **February 17**

AND he said, Verily I say unto you, No prophet is accepted in his own country.   Luke 4:24

Monday — **February 18**

WHEN visiting a big city I like to search out a peaceful corner away from the roaring traffic. I love the quietness that descends, leaving me alone with my thoughts and reflections.

There is a saying, "To the quiet mind all things are possible." I think that's true. In the hush, problems are dissolved, petty cares forgotten.

And when the silence ends and life bursts in once more, we are ready to face its challenges and accept all it has to offer.

Tuesday — **February 19**

FOR all of us whether rich or poor, well or unwell, young or old, the spiritual life is like being cast into a rowing boat in heavy seas.

Fortunately, we have been given a priceless gift. Two oars with which to steer a course; one is called work and the other is prayer.

Wednesday — **February 20**

PETER is a keen golfer. One day, we were talking about the universal appeal the game has when he said:

"You know, Francis, the game of golf has a lot to teach us about how we tackle the game of daily life. You have to concentrate on hitting great shots rather than worrying about bad ones or what others will think if you miss. Just visualise the ball going straight to the target."

Peter has passed on a wonderful recipe for living well.

Thursday — **February 21**

MAY today be there peace within;
May you trust God that you are exactly
where you are meant to be;
May you forget the infinite possibilities that are
born to faith;
May you use those gifts that you have received
And pass on the love given to you.
May you be content knowing you are a child
of God;
Let His presence allow your soul freedom to sing,
dance and turn to the sun.

Friday — **February 22**

FEBRUARY 22nd is Thinking Day for young citizens who belong to organisations like the Brownies and Guides. The date is significant since it was the shared birthday of both Lord and Lady Baden-Powell.

On this day the young people will be encouraged to think about such topics as the happiness provided by a good home, the work of teachers and the medical profession, and their own concern for others worldwide — a commitment to international friendship and understanding.

The Apostle Paul thought that every day should be a Thinking Day. Writing to the Philippians he said, "Whatever things are good and deserve praise: things that are true, noble, right, pure, lovely and honourable, think on these things."

Thinking Day brightens the short and often dark days of February.

Saturday — **February 23**

DAVID and Elizabeth lived busy city lives, but had hopes of early retirement, and moving to a quiet country area. Eventually, they bought a house for their new life and as Elizabeth said:

"It just welcomed us when we went in, and although we were aware both house and garden needed more than a little loving care, we decided it was for us.

"But it wasn't long before we began to wonder if we had been wise," she continued. "As we were living so far away, overseeing the refurbishment wasn't easy."

Then a Winter storm badly damaged the roof, yet at long last they were able to finish the project. "We'll be expecting a visit from you and the Lady of the House — and some gardening advice!" David said.

The Roman poet Horace was right when he wrote: "When the going gets rough, remember to keep calm . . ." — and I'd add, keep going!

Sunday — **February 24**

AND the Word was made flesh, and dwelt among us (and we beheld this glory, the glory as of the only begotten of the Father), full of grace and truth.   John 1:14

Monday — **February 25**

HERE'S some good advice our old friend Mary's grandfather gave to her while she was growing up: "Never live in the past, but always learn from it."

Tuesday — **February 26**

A MOTHER on the bus was shushing her young son: "Don't ask so many questions!" she said.

Of course it can be tiring, even embarrassing, when a child keeps asking things but it's all part of growing up and is how youngsters learn about the world they have come into.

Rudyard Kipling never lost his sense of curiosity, his desire for answers, as this verse of his shows:

I keep six honest serving men
(They taught me all I know);
Their names are What and Why and When
And How and Where and Who.

Wednesday — **February 27**

THE PROMISE

*T*HE trees are still bare, the earth is still mud,
But now, for the first time, new life
is in bud.
Today, high above, the heavens are fair,
The sunshine is bright, and there's warmth
in the air.
Though ruts are still puddles, the sky they reflect
Is blue as a harebell, while verges are decked
With aconites golden, and snowdrops that sway
In breezes that dance the dead Winter away.
Today is a promise, a stirring, a vow,
That Spring will be coming — it won't be
long now!

Margaret Ingall.

Thursday — *February 28*

A REGULAR churchgoer suddenly stopped attending, so some weeks later his clergyman visited him on a chilly evening.

The man, alone at home, guessing the reason for the visit, welcomed him in and invited him to sit by a blazing fire. Then he, too, sat down, waiting. The clergyman sat comfortably, saying nothing but he silently observed the way the flames played around the burning logs.

After some minutes, the clergyman picked up the fire tongs, and carefully lifted out a brightly-burning ember, placing it to one side of the hearth all alone. Then he sat back in his chair, still silent. His host watched all this in quiet fascination.

As the lonely ember's flame diminished, it glowed momentarily and then its fire was gone. Not a word had been spoken since the initial greeting and the two men sat on in reflective silence.

Later the clergyman, about to leave, picked up the cold, dead ember and placed it back into the middle of the fire. Instantly it began to glow once more with the light and warmth of the burning coals around it.

Reaching the door the host said, "Thank you so much for your visit and especially for the fiery sermon! I shall be back in church next Sunday."

Friday — *February 29*

H E who does not wish for little things does not deserve big things.

Belgian Proverb.

March

WHEN, in the early years of the 1900s, John Flynn chose to train as a Presbyterian minister, he may have feared his opportunities for spreading the Good News would be somewhat limited. He was living in the Australian Outback, where the distance between settlements sometimes made it difficult to be of practical help to communities.

However, John was determined to do what he could, and one of his earliest acts was to compile a book called "The Bushman's Companion", a work full of realistic advice which proved to be enormously popular. Perhaps his greatest contribution to Outback life came in 1928 when he set up the Flying Doctor Service — a lifesaver to those isolated settlers who suffered injury or illness.

Next time we feel we can't make much difference in the world, remember John Flynn. We should never give up trying new ideas, whether we happen to live Down Under or Up Over!

COME unto me, all ye that labour and are heavy laden, and I will give you rest.

Matthew 11:28

Monday — **March 3**

HERE is a native American tale. A Cherokee was teaching his grandson about life.

"A struggle is going on inside me," he said to the youngster. "It is a tough one and it is between two wolves. One is evil — he is envy, greed, guilt, resentment, self-pity, lies, and false pride. The other is goodness — he is joy, serenity, humility, benevolence, truth and compassion.

"The same fight is going on inside you and inside every other person, too."

"But tell me, which wolf will win?" the grandson asked.

"The one you feed," came the reply.

Tuesday — **March 4**

SEE the second hand move swiftly
  And the minutes speeding on,
Then the hours passing quickly,
  All too soon the day has gone.
Always moving, sure and steady,
  Certain as the endless tide,
Father Time is not your master
  Let him always be your guide.
Think of those whose days go slowly,
  Those whose moments creep along,
Think of all the lost and lonely
  Offer hope to make them strong.
Watch the minute hand still moving
  As the hours slip away,
Use each precious moment wisely,
  Make the most of every day!
                    Iris Hesselden.

Wednesday — **March 5**

THE Archbishop of York, John Sentamu from Uganda, was for a time Bishop of Stepney where he won hearts with his simplicity and warm humanity.

Once, when he was walking along a damp street, a little girl stopped him. "Mister, will you tie my shoelace?"

"Of course," he said, and knelt on the pavement to do so. As he finished the child patted him on the head. "That's a good boy," she said.

With a chuckle he recalled, "I thought it was the greatest compliment anyone had ever paid me!"

Thursday — **March 6**

ARE you undecided about trying to start a new project? If so, perhaps you would like to reflect on these words written by Sidney Smith:

"A great deal of talent is lost to the world for want of a little courage."

Friday — **March 7**

BE gentle when you touch bread:
Let it not lie uncared for and unwanted;
Too often bread is taken for granted.
There is such beauty in bread:
Beauty of the sun and soil,
Beauty of patient toil,
Wind and rain have caressed it,
Christ often blessed it.
Be gentle when you touch bread.
Anon.

Saturday — **March 8**

THE wind had been howling all night and the Lady of the House and I wondered what damage had been done to our garden. Sure enough, at first glance before breakfast I saw the contents of three large plant pots spilled across the path.

I dressed in my warmest clothes, preparing to find out what else had happened. When I reached the front door there was mail on the mat. Opening the door I saw the postman's reflective jacket disappearing into the gloom . . . and the three plant pots neatly back where they belonged.

The rest of my day was enriched by that one unspoken act and the words of the German poet Matthias Claudius came to mind: "Good deeds done silently and for a good motive — they are the flowers that withstand the storm!"

Sunday — **March 9**

FOR we know that if our earthly house of this tabernacle were dissolved, we have a building of God, an house not made with hands, eternal in the heavens.

Corinthians II: 5:1

Monday — **March 10**

KATHLEEN'S five-year-old niece Hannah saw a sliver of rainbow peeking through the clouds one afternoon and exclaimed, "Look — there's a little piece of heaven!"

Sometimes it takes a child to remind us how close God really is.

COMING ALIVE

Tuesday — **March 11**

THE author of these lines is unknown to me but, having read the words, I feel I know all I need to about his or her heart.

Have you leant upon a gate, without a
*   need for words,*
To take in Nature's wonder and to listen
*   to the birds?*
Yes, leaning on a gate is a thing we ought
*   to do.*
It helps us to unwind and such moments
*   are so few.*

Wednesday — **March 12**

HOWEVER much we love someone,
*   It's hard but very true,*
We cannot live their lives for them,
*   Or turn their grey skies blue.*

For sometimes we must stand apart,
*   And let them go their way,*
To walk a path, or make a choice
*   In which we have no say.*

Yet though our helpless hearts may fret,
*   When dear ones seem so frail,*
Remember, there is still a Power
*   Whose strength will never fail.*

For those we love are never lost,
*   E'en though we can't be there,*
The Lord keeps track of every one,
*   And holds them in His care.*

Margaret Ingall.

Thursday — *March 13*

WALT Disney died before Disney World was opened to the public and his widow was asked to take part in the special ceremony to mark the occasion. When an official said to her, "I wish Walt could have seen this," Mrs Disney replied, "He did."

Vision is the ability to see and believe in the intangible — it's hope fulfilled because of faith and perseverance. As Hebrews 10:35 says, "Therefore do not cast away your confidence, which has great reward."

Friday — *March 14*

JANET had a dozen red roses delivered to her one day with an accompanying card which said, "From someone who loves you." That was all.

Being single, she wondered if a secret admirer was behind this delightful and intriguing surprise. Or could it be someone in her family?

Janet went through a list of people she knew, but finally, in exasperation, she called her sister Doreen and asked: "Did you, by any chance, send me flowers?"

"Yes," came the reply.

"Why?" asked a puzzled Janet.

"Well," Doreen said, "You sounded so fed up last time we talked, so I just wanted you to spend one whole day thinking about all the people who care about you so much."

This is a story to put new heart into those who think the world has been passing them by.

Saturday — **March 15**

MOST of us, I'm sad to say, wouldn't have to look very far to find someone who "bore a grudge". Sometimes the slightest of grievances can harden hearts for years. Consider these words by André Maurois:

"Often we allow ourselves to be upset by small things we should despise and forget. Perhaps someone we helped has proved ungrateful, or someone we believed our friend has spoken ill of us. We feel such disappointments so deeply we can no longer work or sleep.

"But consider that we have so few years to live and we are losing irreplaceable hours brooding over such grievances — grievances so small that they would soon be forgotten by everyone else! Let us then devote our time and energy to worthwhile deeds, to great things, warm affections and enduring actions.

"For life is too short to be too little."

Sunday — **March 16**

THEREFORE turn thou to thy God: keep mercy and judgment, and wait on thy God continually.
Hosea 12:6

Monday — **March 17**

THE annual celebration of St. Patrick's Day on 17th March reminds me of this cheerful wish passed on some years ago by friends in the Emerald Isle:

May you live as long as you want, and never want as long as you live.

TIME AND TIDE

Tuesday — *March 18*

I DOUBT if any of us will get through this life without knowing loss and the pain of bereavement. In Henry Scott Holland's poem "Death Is Nothing At All" the one who has passed away speaks to loved ones left behind:

Let my name be ever the household word
*   that it always was.*
Let it be spoken without effort,
Without the ghost of a shadow in it.
Life means all that it ever meant.
It is the same as it ever was;
There is absolute unbroken continuity.
What is death but a negligible accident?
Why should I be out of mind
Because I am out of sight?
I am waiting for you for an interval,
Somewhere very near,
Just around the corner.
All is well.

Wednesday — *March 19*

HERE are two sayings to keep in mind, not just today but every day of the year:

There is an island of opportunity in the middle of every difficulty.

Give to the world the best you have and the best will come back to you.

Thursday — *March 20*

CHEESE, wine and a friend must be old to be good.

Cuban Proverb.

Friday — **March 21**

THE poet John Clare wrote these lines in celebration of Spring. They remind us that while we might have changed with the years, the important things in life are still the same. I hope we'll always have enough Spring in our hearts to see them.

The daisy looks up in my face
As long ago it smiled;
It knows no change but keeps its place
And takes me for a child.

Saturday — **March 22**

JOE, who's a keen coin collector, showed me a picture of an old Spanish coin. Engraved on the coin were the Pillars of Hercules, the gateway between the Mediterranean and the unexplored Atlantic Ocean. It bore the inscription *Ne Plus Ultra*, meaning No More Beyond.

Eventually Columbus sailed across the ocean and found America. The coins had to be recast and later versions simply read *Plus Ultra*.

It took a brave man to lead the way from one continent to another, but it took a unique man to lead the way from this world to the next. In dying and rising again for our sins Jesus proved there was indeed *Plus Ultra*, or More Beyond.

Sunday — **March 23**

AND when Jesus had cried with a loud voice, he said, Father, into thy hands I commend my spirit: and having said thus, he gave up the ghost.
Luke 23:46

IN PASTURES GREEN

Monday — *March 24*

OUR friend Sam has never forgotten these lines which hung on the wall of his Aunt Grace's sitting-room:

You cannot set the whole world right,
Nor all the people in it:
You cannot do the work of years in just
*   a single minute;*
But keep one little corner straight,
By humble, patient labour
And do the work that each hour brings —
And help your next-door neighbour.

Tuesday — *March 25*

THERE were once two soldiers who became prisoners-of-war. Both were treated with great cruelty. War ended at last and the soldiers returned home. During an interview, a journalist asked them if they could ever forgive their captors. One said, "No, never. I shall never forgive or forget."

The other turned to him and said quietly, "Then you are still in prison."

Wednesday — *March 26*

THE Lady of the House received these words in a best wishes card sent across the miles from Georgia in the USA, and I'd like to share the thought with you today:

I asked for a flower, He gave me a garden;
I asked for a tree, He gave me a forest;
I asked for a river, He gave me an ocean;
I asked for a friend, He gave me you.

Thursday — *March 27*

WOULD you like to be seen as a wise person? Would you like your judgement to be sought by others? Years of book learning won't necessarily help, but according to the Mabinogion, a collection of ancient Welsh tales, the answer is really quite simple.

"The three foundations of Judgement are — bold design, constant practice and frequent mistakes."

So don't let your mistakes and miscalculations pull you down; appreciate them instead, for they prove you're on the right road after all.

Friday — *March 28*

WE all enjoy stories which reflect how famous people are only human like the rest of us. And how much better when they themselves join in the laughter!

Albert Einstein may have been the world's foremost physicist and mathematician, but he was no violin player. He recalled the frustration felt by his musical partner during one particular duet.

"Albert, it's in waltz time. All you have to do is count one, two, three, one, two, three. Surely you can count to three, Albert!"

And the author William Golding, of "Lord Of The Flies" fame, recounts an encounter he had with a traffic warden. Pointing at the No Parking sign she shouted, "Can't you read?"

The irate official might have chosen different words had she seen Golding the previous week receiving the Nobel Prize for Literature.

Saturday — **March 29**

I ALWAYS have mixed feelings when I see a furniture van and signs of a household on the move.

On the one hand I feel a tinge of sadness as I think of the empty house left behind and the bare rooms. But I think, too, of the life ahead, new rooms waiting to be transformed into a home. I say a silent prayer that the family or the person — whoever they are — will fill these rooms with laughter and memories to cherish.

If the home is the heart of the nation, as has been said, then every new and happy home enriches us all.

Sunday — **March 30**

AND the angel of the Lord appeared unto him and said unto him, The Lord is with thee, thou mighty man of valour.   Judges 6:12

Monday — **March 31**

A CORRESPONDENT in Scotland came across this "Rule Of Life" and she thought others would like to share its wise words:

I am: I ought: I can: I will.

I am a child of God.

I ought to do my duty because God made me in His image.

I can do my best because God has given me four things: A body to work with. A mind to think with. A soul to love with. A will to choose with.

I will, by God's grace, always try to do what He would wish me to do.

April

*I'M just a fool for April
I love each tender day,
More kind than March's mayhem,
   Less bold than teasing May,
Sweet April's wild and lovely,
   With eyes as bright as rain,
She's graceful as the bluebells
   That bloom in every lane.
She startles in an instant,
   Her smiles may turn to tears,
But when she laughs, a little glimpse
   Of Summer's joy appears.*

                                    Margaret Ingall.

A NATIONAL newspaper once received a letter from one of its readers asking the question "What's wrong with the world?"

A few days later the paper printed a reply from the author G. K. Chesterton. It read:

Dear Sir,

   What's wrong with the world?
   I am.

He had hit on a truth rarely recognised. If the world has ills, it is we who have created them and we who must work to put them right.

Thursday — *April 3*

THE verse-speaking class for children was over. Young Robert marched up confidently to collect the winner's certificate from the judges.

He paused only long enough to shake hands, then off he went without a word to join his mother, good manners forgotten in his excitement.

A gentle reminder of "thank you!" came from the platform but no-one in the hall expected Robert's cheerful response.

"You're welcome!" he cried, without stopping. No doubt he wondered why everyone began to laugh . . .

Friday — *April 4*

LIFE is a series of bridges —
Bridges we need to cross over,
Sometimes, they welcome the wanderer home
And sometimes, they beckon the rover.
Bridges from here to tomorrow,
With links from the past to today,
And always a journey of spirit
Still seeking and finding the way.

Bridges of love and of friendship,
So often in need of repair,
A place to renew and replenish,
Rebuilding with hope and with care.
Life is a bridge to the future,
Eternity just out of sight,
So cross all your bridges with courage,
Reach out to the love and the light.

Iris Hesselden.

Saturday — *April 5*

HERE are two unusual ways of looking at this new, fresh Spring season.

Leigh Hunt, the essayist, asks, "Suppose flowers themselves were new. Suppose they had just come into this world, a sweet reward for some new goodness."

Can you imagine how we would stop and stare?

Then the poet Henry Wadsworth Longfellow suggests: "If Spring came but once a century instead of once a year, or burst forth with the sound of an earthquake and not in silence, what wonder and expectation there would be in all hearts to behold the miraculous change."

Sunday — *April 6*

AND whosoever shall compel thee to go a mile, go with him twain.   Matthew 5:41

Monday — *April 7*

AS the character J.R. Ewing in the television series "Dallas", Larry Hagman had a sneering attitude to all that was good. His only pleasure seemed to come from other people's misery. But the actor who portrayed that character has a completely different philosophy in real life — and reinforces it each morning!

"My credo is etched on my bathroom mirror," Larry says, "and I see it when I brush my teeth in the morning. It says, *Don't Worry, Be Happy, Feel Good*. When you see that first thing in the morning, and you reflect on it, the rest of the day seems to glide by pretty well."

Tuesday — **April 8**

IN the land of the glacier-cut fjords and giant moss-draped cedars of the Great Bear Rain Forest in British Columbia, a myth is told by the Gitga'at people explaining the presence of black bears with a rare gene which makes some of them snow-white.

The Raven Deity, it is said, swooped down at the end of an ice age and decided that a tenth of black bears would be bleached as "spirit bears", a reminder to future generations that they must keep the world pure.

A few years ago, local officials, Native Canadian nations, logging companies and environmentalists announced an agreement to designate five million acres to be preserved in the home of the spirit bear, an area which is also the world's largest remaining intact temperate coastal rainforest.

This is aimed at future preservation of not only the few hundred spirit bears and other black bears but also a large number of grizzly bears, goshawks, deer, wolves and mountain goats.

"There's a new era dawning," the Province's Premier Gordon Campbell said at the time. "You have to establish what you value and work together."

Wednesday — **April 9**

THESE points to ponder were seen on a church notice board not long ago:
Let go and let God.
God = Good Orderly Direction.
Learn to listen and listen to learn.

CLOUDLESS DAY

*Thursday — **April 10***

" **I**F you want happiness for an hour; take a nap. If you want happiness for a day; go fishing. If you want happiness for a year; inherit a fortune. If you want happiness for a lifetime; help someone." Chinese Proverb.

*Friday — **April 11***

BREATH OF SPRING

*B*REEZES share the Winter's bite
  As young buds shiver still.
But I see sunlight flicker
  On struggling daffodils.
They sway as if to music
  And rustle in the breeze.
There can be none so graceful
  Or beautiful as these.
And daisies in their hundreds
  Lie white upon the grass,
Inviting every butterfly
  To linger when they pass.
I hear Winter weeping as
  The swollen buds break free;
And roses sweetly blushing
  As they were meant to be.
These flowers are His treasures;
  His footprints leave a train
Of beauty and of wonder,
  We see time and again.
Grey days are surely over.
  Now new life can begin.
Look up and see the sunshine.
  And feel the breath of Spring.
          Mo Crawshaw.

Saturday — *April 12*

DO you know these lines from Tennyson's "In Memoriam"? I thought I would share them with you today. Don't they wish something wonderful for all of us, and encourage us to help bring it about?

Ring in the valiant man and free
The larger heart, the kindlier hand;
Ring out the darkness of the land,
Ring in the Christ that is to be.

Sunday — *April 13*

THIS is the bread which cometh down from heaven, that a man may eat thereof, and not die. John 6:50

Monday — *April 14*

TIME is a gift. It may be said to come in a wooden chest containing three drawers. The bottom drawer is deep and full, a bit of a clutter, for it contains the stored-up memories of all our yesterdays.

The middle drawer is sealed tight, for it holds who knows what? The secrets of tomorrow.

The top drawer contains the coinage of today, each pennyworth of time to be spent with wisdom, generosity and love, for the way we use these precious coins determines the contents of the other two.

These three drawers are then linked by the chest surrounding them. Without any one, it would be incomplete.

Tuesday — *April 15*

I ONCE met a politician who was famous for delivering inspirational speeches. After he addressed a packed hall, I asked him how long it had taken to write that particular speech.

"The writing took only an hour," he replied gently, then with a wry smile he added, "But the experience took a lifetime."

Wednesday — *April 16*

I'VE learned about a wonderful garden at Bridgham in Norfolk; William Fairbank's Garden of Peace. This creation, also called Bridgham Sculpture Park, is in William's own wild garden, where he has planted many varieties of trees, from graceful birch to sturdy oak. A skilled carpenter and sculptor in wood, he was involved in a serious accident in 1987.

Creating a Garden of Peace was part of William's personal healing process. In it are abstract wooden sculptures which he hopes will inspire in those who visit a sense of spiritual renewal. It took William seven years to create his unique Stations of the Cross, the Forest Stations: carved from wood from all over the world, they have been exhibited in many churches.

William Fairbank likes people, whatever their faith, to come and visit his work. Perhaps it will help them to find time to reflect in a busy world. He believes individual peace leads, in turn, to universal peace — "Every village should have a place for world peace where one can come and be, whatever one's religion."

Thursday — *April 17*

WE'VE all heard the expression, "God loves a cheerful giver". But it took some time for me to realise the full force behind these words.

Beverly Sills was an American opera singer, but she is also known as "the special mother to special children". The mother of two children who were born with disabilities, she used her fame to raise many millions of dollars to help families in the same position.

When asked about happiness she replied, "I'm not happy, I'm cheerful. There's a difference. A happy woman has no cares at all. A cheerful woman has cares but has learned how to deal with them."

Perhaps the Lord loves a cheerful giver more because He sees the pain in the heart that makes the smile so much more precious.

Friday — *April 18*

WHO would think that kittens could teach us how to live? Florence Nightingale once introduced two kittens to a home where an elderly tom cat was already in residence. He didn't like the intrusion.

"As he ran at them," Miss Nightingale wrote, "The bigger and handsomer kitten ran away, but the littler one stood her ground and, when her old enemy came close enough, kissed his nose to make the peace."

This tale reminded me of Abraham Lincoln, who said, "Do I not destroy my enemies when I make them my friends?"

Saturday — **April 19**

OUR friend Alice is into recycling in a big way. Garden waste goes to make compost, bottles and jars go to the bottlebank and into other "banks" go old clothes and newspapers.

If all these things can be renewed, why not ourselves, too? We can cut out our negative thoughts and make room in our minds for new, positive ones. We can take our bad habits and change them into good ones.

Our lives can be recycled just like the old clothes and bottles.

Sunday — **April 20**

AND immediately he received his sight, and followed him, glorifying God: and all the people, when they saw it, gave praise unto God.

Luke 18:43

Monday — **April 21**

IN the nineteenth century, women in America were not expected to hold strong political views. If they did they had to keep quiet.

Lucy Stone rebelled against this. Coming from a traditional Massachusetts family she shocked society by speaking out on women's rights.

When she openly opposed slavery she was urged not to get involved. She gave this answer:

"If in this hour of the world's need I should refuse to lend my aid, however small it may be, I should have no right to think myself a Christian."

When slavery was finally abolished it was thanks to courageous spirits like Lucy.

Tuesday — *April 22*

THERE'S a line in Leonard Cohen's song, "Anthem" which cheers up Colin when he feels he's done less than his best, when he hasn't quite lived up to the ideals he set for his life.

"There is a crack, a crack in everything," is how this seemingly hopeless line begins. However, it ends ". . . that's how the light gets in."

It reminds us that it's only because of our shortcomings that the Light of Christ came into the world. It's through our very flaws that He enters our lives. Then it's up to us to let Him shine out again.

Wednesday — *April 23*

JOY and the Lady of the House have been close friends since childhood. Joy married and moved to Florida, then Switzerland, finally settling in New Zealand.

Over the years Joy and the Lady of the House wrote to each other; and each treasures a huge box of letters. They seldom have the chance to see each other nowadays but when they have occasionally met, it's as though they're young again.

Like a precious box of old letters, true friendship endures. Time cannot erase its substance.

Thursday — *April 24*

HOW far that little candle throws his beams! So shines a good deed in a weary world.

William Shakespeare.

Friday — *April 25*

OUR old friend Mary came across an interview with Dora Bryan, the much-loved actress who has starred not only in films, but several West End musicals. Like many people in the entertainment industry, she has a deep and abiding faith which has helped her cope with the many highs and lows she has experienced over the years.

"I do love hymns," she is quoted as saying. "They see the reality of life in such a simple and vivid way."

One hymn of which her words immediately reminded me is "How Can I Keep From Singing?" written in the 19th century by Robert Lowry:

. . . Through all the tumult and the strife
I hear the music ringing;
It finds an echo in my soul —
How can I keep from singing?

Glorious and uplifting words which do indeed see "the reality of life".

Saturday — *April 26*

ANN, a reader in Brussels, sent our friend Alison this recipe for living which seems to say a lot in a few words:

Enjoy life, respect nature and don't forget to think of others' needs.

Sunday — *April 27*

SURELY goodness and mercy shall follow me all the days of my life: and I will dwell in the house of the Lord for ever.   Psalms 23:6

Monday — *April 28*

HERE is a good thought to keep in mind at the start of a new week: *Even more important than a friendly meeting is a friendly parting.*

Tuesday — *April 29*

MY friend, Andrew, has had an interesting life. Twice since I've known him he has worked his way from unemployment, through humdrum jobs and into senior positions. Each time his situation took a turn for the worse his friends knew it wouldn't be long until he was on the up again.

His secret, I'm sure, is contained in a framed poem that hangs in his workshop. It's by E. A. Guest:

To live as gently as I can;
To be, no matter what, a man;
To take what comes of good or ill
And cling to faith and honour still;
To do my best and let that stand
The record of my brain and hand;
And then, should failure come to me,
Still work and hope for victory.

Wednesday — *April 30*

TWO stonecutters were asked what they were doing. The first said, "I'm cutting this stone into blocks."

The second man replied, "I'm a member of a team building a new hospital."

It all depends how you look at life.

May

Thursday — **May 1**

IN a world where differences of opinion can sometimes crop up, it's good to remind ourselves that we are all, each and every one of us, part of a larger family. The great humanitarian, Albert Schweitzer, said: "You don't live in this world alone. Your brothers and sisters are here, too."

And, as the poet and politician Alphonse de Lamartine pointed out: "If God is thy father, Human beings are thy brothers and sisters."

Friday — **May 2**

WE all know the Victorians built houses to last, but what about their homes? I came across these words on a card which seem to show that the Victorians, rulers of a vast empire, relied on a greater Power for true happiness and fulfilment. You surely won't go far wrong in the twenty-first century if you follow this blueprint:

Can you tell me how to build a happy home?

Integrity must be the Architect, Tidiness the Upholsterer. It must be warmed by affection, lighted up by cheerfulness.

Industry must be the ventilator. But the greatest requisite of all is The Sunshine From Above.

Saturday — *May 3*

ON the other side of the world tomorrow is "Midori no hi"; translated from Japanese that means "Greenery Day". People of all ages will try to spend time out of doors, in gardens, playing in parks or just walking in the countryside. I have heard it described as, "a day to commune with nature and to be thankful".

A lovely idea, I'm sure you'll agree. But why limit it to just one day when there are so many days to choose from?

It needn't be a full-blown ramble, it may only be half an hour sitting on your patio, but there's nothing like a breath of fresh air and the sun on your face to make a person glad to be alive.

Go on, have a Greenery Day!

Sunday — *May 4*

LAY up for yourselves treasures in heaven, where neither moth nor rust doth corrupt.

Matthew 6:20

Monday — *May 5*

THE qualities asked for in this poem by Henry Vaughan seem simple enough. But look again — the secret of true happiness lies here.

Give me humility and peace,
Contented thoughts, innocuous ease,
A sweet, revengeless, quiet mind,
Be to my greatest haters, kind
Give me, my God, a heart as mild
And plain as when I was a child.

*Tuesday — **May 6***

JIMMY is a retired farm worker. For over forty-five years he worked hard and enjoyed it. He now lives quietly, carving beautiful walking sticks with rams' horn handles in his spare time and giving them away to anyone who shows an interest in them.

But would you call Jimmy a successful man? I'd say so, and so would the American writer Maya Angelou. "Success" — for her (and Jimmy) — "is liking yourself, liking what you do and liking how you do it."

*Wednesday — **May 7***

DAYBREAK

A WALK while day is dawning is a blessing,
  A draught of water for the thirsty soul;
Beneath a gallant sun intent on dressing
  A rain-washed tattered sky in sheets of gold,
I deeply drink as morning light unfolds.

The rose and gilded clouds are barely dry,
  Mirrored puddles glitter at my feet,
And baby birds peer from their perches high
  While parents gossip somewhere in the trees
Of stormy rumbles carried on the breeze.

Oh! In moments fashioned such as this,
  Tenderly, from Mother Nature's breast,
There is no earthly place of greater bliss
  Or hall in heaven holding sweeter rest
Than a walk in daybreak's splendidness.

Rachel Wallace-Oberle.

Thursday — *May 8*

GRAEME is a keen photographer, but though he enjoys taking pictures of stunning scenery, he's just as keen to take his camera to the cities and suburbs of the world.

"There are wonderful things to be seen everywhere," he said one day as he showed me his latest shots. "Beauty might seem more obvious in the countryside, but actually it's just as evident in human activities and faces."

Graeme's wise words put me in mind of Emily Dickinson's verse:

Who has not found the heaven below
Will fail of it above.
God's residence is next to mine,
His furniture is love.

Friday — *May 9*

MAY the hearth be gladdened
By the laughter of children,
By the kinship of clan,
By the wisdom of elders,
By the memory of souls passed,
By the joy of souls yet to be born,
No remembrance of sorrow to darken the day
But songs, smiles and stories to brighten
the gathering,
And the presence of Christ to share our delight.
(Celtic Blessing for a family gathering.)

Saturday — *May 10*

A GOOD example is like a bell that calls many to church.
Danish Proverb.

Sunday — **May 11**

MY love be with you all in Christ Jesus. Amen.
Corinthians I 16:24

Monday — **May 12**

CLEARING out some children's story books Lyn inevitably found herself beginning to re-read some of them. Her favourite tale was about a sad little squirrel who had lost her bounce. She moped around the forest floor, until her friend the rabbit noticed.

"What's wrong?" Rabbit asked.

"I'm so unhappy," Squirrel replied. "I can't hop like you, I can't tunnel like Mole, and I can't swim like Otter. I can't do anything and I'm no use to anyone." She hid her head and cried.

"But, Squirrel," cried Rabbit. "You have such a beautiful tail! We all love watching you dancing along with it flying gracefully behind you."

Squirrel looked at her reflection in the pond and realised that Rabbit was right. She cheered up immediately.

"Oh, Rabbit," she beamed, "Thank you for making me realise that there is something special about me after all!" And she scampered off happily through the forest, displaying her fluffy tail behind her.

It's a charming children's story, and I think we can learn from it. We all have something special about us, and we must constantly remind ourselves of this. Even m ore importantly, we must be like Rabbit, and notice and appreciate others' good points.

WELCOME!

Tuesday — *May 13*

WHERE would we be without the telephone? From the days when operators would get to know their clients so well that they would act as babysitter to a child sleeping beside a phone left off the hook, or call to remind someone it was time to take a cake out the oven, to modern text messaging, this means of communication has played a major role in our lives.

Prompted, perhaps, by hearing the engaged tone once too often, Edith Armstrong wrote these wise words about her own approach to living a happy life:

"I keep the telephone of my mind open," she said, "to peace, harmony, health, love, and abundance. Then, whenever doubt, anxiety, or fear try to call me, they will keep getting a busy signal and soon they'll forget my number."

Wednesday — *May 14*

A READER has sent me "A Collector's Prayer", written with Christian Aid Week in mind:
Lord of life,
Underneath me are two feet —
Please may they do this task willingly;
In front of me are rows of doors —
Please may they open to me cheerfully;
In my hand are dozens of envelopes —
Please may they be filled generously;
In my heart are millions of needy people —
May all I do this week make this a world in
* which they can thrive.*
            Amen.

Thursday — **May 15**

FRED had been on holiday, so I was keen to find out how he'd enjoyed it.

"Well," he said, "you know how busy my job is, so I decided to go on a week's walking tour by myself. The first day was wonderful, the second and third were not quite so good, and by the last day I just couldn't wait to see everyone again."

His story reminded me of some words of St Thomas Aquinas, who wrote: "Friendship is the source of the greatest pleasures; without friends even the most agreeable pursuits become tedious."

"I second that," said Fred. "In fact, next time I decide to go anywhere by myself, I'm going to make sure I take some friends with me!"

Friday — **May 16**

WHEN the storms of life are raging
The future looking dark,
Keep that ray of hope within you
    Keep alive that little spark.
When your problems all beset you
    Wonder where should you begin?
Seek the promise of the rainbow
    And the hope deep down within.
When you feel you are deserted
    Or your friends forget to call,
Then cherish all your memories
    For love can conquer all.
When skies are grey and cloudy
    Or you're feeling insecure,
Let that ray of hope sustain you
    And start afresh once more.
                    Iris Hesselden.

Saturday — **May 17**

HERE are a few wise and thoughtful words from the eighteenth-century man of letters, Dr Samuel Johnson.

"A friend may be often found and lost, but an old friend never can be found, and nature has provided that he cannot easily be lost."

Sunday — **May 18**

THEN David arose from the earth, and washed, and anointed himself, and changed his apparel, and came into the house of the Lord, and worshipped.   Samuel II 12:20

Monday — **May 19**

LEAD us, heavenly Father, lead us
O'er the world's tempestuous sea;
Guard us, guide us, keep us, feed us,
For we have no help but thee.

Simple words and familiar ones, too. Their author was James Edmeston, eminent architect, loyal friend of the London Orphan Asylum and committed to the welfare of children, for whom many of his hymns were written. Latterly churchwarden of St Barnabas in Homerton, he wrote a new hymn each Sunday and read it at family worship.

This wasn't his only claim to fame. As an architect, one of his students was Sir George Gilbert Scott, whose work can still be seen today — from the splendour of London's Albert Memorial to Glasgow University and Edinburgh's Episcopal Cathedral.

Tuesday — *May 20*

JUST THE TONIC!

TRY out a smile when you're down in the dumps
And the world seems so dreary and grey;
Laugh at the clouds, when the sky's in a mood,
And you'll frighten the raindrops away!
Look on the bright side of life when you can,
For surely it just goes to show,
By thinking that way, you'll be finding each day
The bright side's the best side to know!

Elizabeth Gozney.

Wednesday — *May 21*

THE author C. S. Lewis once said, "You can't get a cup of tea big enough or a book long enough to suit me."

Our friend Paul has framed and hung this quote above his desk as a reminder to set aside some quiet moments:

When life gets hectic, we tend to neglect the little things we enjoy most. How important it is to remember that simple pleasures refresh the spirit and nurture the soul.

Thursday — *May 22*

SOMEONE once said to a clergyman who was sitting relaxing and enjoying summer sunshine in his garden, "If only God would perform a miracle before my very eyes, I could believe in Him."

The clergyman said nothing. He simply bent down, plucked a blade of grass and silently held it out to the visitor.

Friday — *May 23*

AFTER many years in Africa the missionary David Livingstone addressed a gathering in Glasgow. The audience might well have been shocked at his gaunt appearance — his arm hung limply by his side after being mauled by a lion. This was a man who had faced many challenges and a great deal of hardship.

Asked what kept him going through years of privation, thousands of miles from home, he replied, "Just this — 'Lo, I am with you always, even unto the ends of the world.' On these words I staked everything, and they never failed."

Help not just for heroes in far-flung places but for every one of us wherever we might be.

Saturday — *May 24*

WORK while you work,
Play while you play,
One thing each time,
That is the way.
All that you do,
Do with your might —
Things done by halves
Are never done right.

Anon.

Sunday — *May 25*

AND he said unto them, Cast the net on the right side of the ship, and ye shall find. They cast therefore, and now they were not able to draw it for the multitude of fishes.

John 21:6

THE FRIENDSHIP BOOK

Monday — *May 26*

WHAT do you think of when you first wake in the morning? Perhaps your mind dwells on what you have to do that day, or what the weather is to be like.

Neil once told me what his first thought is. "I say good morning to the morning," he said. "And I look forward to whatever it has in store. To me every new day is a gift. I wouldn't dream of not wishing it good morning!"

Is it any wonder Neil is one of the most contented people I know?

Tuesday — *May 27*

HERE is a thought-provoking quote from Jonas Salk, famous for the part he played in perfecting the polio vaccine:

"Our greatest responsibility is to be good ancestors."

Wednesday — *May 28*

OF course we all want to succeed in what we try to do, but what if we don't achieve success?

When I was young I took part in a race I hoped to win, but instead I was well and truly beaten.

Seeing my disappointment, our sports teacher came over and said, "Being a winner is easy. Learning how to lose is a lot harder. Now, take one big swallow and enter your name for the next race."

One big swallow . . . I have done it often since. Try it. It's simple — and it works!

CAPTURE THE
MOMENT

Thursday — **May 29**

IT is easy to put your foot in it. We all say, at some time, something we wish we hadn't.

That is why I keep, in a corner at the back of my mind, this little gem: "Always choose tasteful words — you might have to eat them later."

Friday — **May 30**

A WONDERFUL thing, the
  Philosopher's Stone —
Or that's how the legend is told.
  Its magical power can conjure up wealth,
By turning base metal to gold.

Now, though I'd agree that this mythical Stone
  May sound like a rather good tool,
There is, all around us, a simpler device
  Which brings truer riches to all.

We know it as Friendship — it's real and it's free,
  No secrets of cash does it hold,
Just gifts to enrich every day of your life
  With pleasures more precious than gold!
                                    Margaret Ingall.

Saturday — **May 31**

WE all know that those who expect the worst in people or places will usually find it, while people who expect the opposite . . . Well, Harriet Beecher Stowe, the author of "Uncle Tom's Cabin", put it better than I ever could:

"The unthankful heart discovers no mercies; but let the thankful heart sweep through the day and, as the magnet finds the iron, so it will find in every hour some heavenly blessings."

June

ALSO I heard the voice of the Lord, saying, Whom shall I send, and who will go for us? Then said I, Here am I; send me.   Isaiah 6:8

TODAY I'd like to share with you this delightful poem by one of our regular contributors:

Forever overflowing
  With love and life and light,
With joy to lift the morning clouds
  And chase away the night.
With bounty meant for all the world,
  For people everywhere,
God's basket filled with hope and peace
  And endless loving care.

With all the beauty of the earth
  Replenished day by day,
And all the precious gifts of life
  To help us on our way.
Forever overflowing
  With blessings from above,
With faith and hope for us to share,
  God's basket, filled with love.

                    Iris Hesselden.

Tuesday — *June 3*

WALKING through town our friend Margaret was surprised to overhear a young woman call out cheerfully to her friend, "We've plenty of time — I've just bought three hours!"

Soon she realised that the woman was referring to her car-parking ticket but, all the same, Margaret couldn't help thinking how wonderful it would be if we could go to a machine and buy extra time.

Sadly, of course, life isn't like that. We can't just purchase five more minutes to get to the bus-stop, an hour in which to write letters, or even a whole day to catch up on gardening. This surely makes it all the more important that we value the time we do have. As writer Denis Waitley points out:

". . . time is amazingly fair and forgiving. No matter how much time you've wasted in the past, you still have an entire tomorrow."

Let's make the most of it!

Wednesday — *June 4*

THERE was a famous poster during the Second World War which said "Careless Talk Costs Lives". It was a warning that a piece of vital information might reach enemy ears.

There is still such a thing as careless talk, but in a different context. Rumours are repeated and can become ever more colourful and damaging. Reputations are tarnished. Events are described in such a way as to show someone in a bad light.

There is only one way to treat such "careless talk". Stop it!

Thursday — **June 5**

THE happiest people don't necessarily have the best of everything — they just make the most of everything that comes their way.

Friday — **June 6**

HOW many of us have found the A-Z street maps invaluable in finding our way about? These were all due to one amazing woman.

Phyllis Pearsall, deceptively small and frail, lived a somewhat Bohemian life as a writer and traveller and in 1935, when lost in London and trying to use a 20-year-old street map, she was inspired to plot and list another one.

Her father, who owned a mapping business, loaned James Duncan to assist her in the massive undertaking. Incredibly in 1936 she walked every street in London, rising at 5.00 a.m., working an eighteen-hour day and covering 3000 miles.

When completed, the first edition nearly omitted Trafalgar Square altogether after an accident with a shoebox which contained the "Tr" entries! Forming the Geographer's A-Z Map Company, Phyllis had 10,000 copies printed, completing all the proof reading and design work herself.

Phyllis' A-Z map proved to be a great success and years later the idea was extended to produce maps for places such as Birmingham, Liverpool and Edinburgh.

So the next time we reach for an A-Z street map, we can perhaps more fully appreciate this wonderful legacy.

BIRDS OF A FEATHER

Saturday — *June 7*

ACCORDING to our old friend Mary, too many of us are guilty of holding back a suitable word of praise when the deserving person is a member of our own family.

"We are apt to go all the way in thanking or praising total strangers," she said. "Yet we often shy back, somehow, from turning the spotlight on our own relatives."

There's a little-known rhyme that puts it well:
We flatter those we scarcely know,
We please the fleeting guest,
But deal full many a thoughtless blow
To those who love us best.

Sunday — *June 8*

GOD be merciful unto us, and bless us: and cause his face to shine upon us.

Psalms 67:1

Monday — *June 9*

WHAT a great delight is a day of sunshine,
A clear blue sky when the storm is over.

These are the first two lines of that timeless piece of Italian opera, "O Sole Mio". It occurs to me that great songs or poems are rarely written about beautiful days that follow other beautiful days. The storm is what makes the clear blue sky which follows so enjoyable.

That might just be the reason for storms, to help us appreciate the good times, in the same way as the trials and tribulations of life are sent to prepare us for the "great delight" to come.

Tuesday — **June 10**

IT wasn't long since Phil had retired from his job as a primary school headmaster and, perhaps unsurprisingly, he'd been finding it difficult to wind down.

"I was filling every minute at work with so many activities," he said, "that I hardly had a moment to spare for my wife and family — until she came up with a quotation by James Dent:

'A perfect Summer day is when the sun is shining, the breeze is blowing, the birds are singing and the lawn mower is broken'."

I do like quotes which amuse as well as make us reflect — and what an excellent way that is of reminding us that sometimes it's good just to sit back and do nothing but enjoy life.

Wednesday — **June 11**

I KNEEL to say my daily prayer,
All is quiet, still the air,
As ghosts of pilgrims move among
And mingle with the current throng,
Where masons toiled and left their mark,
In nave and cloister grey and stark,
Stain-glassed sunshine filters through,
To dapple choir stall and pew,
Towers soar up to the sky,
With joyous peals that glorify,
And, at the ending of my prayer,
I simply stand in awe and stare,
Where ancient worshippers once trod,
In Durham's monument to God.

Brian H. Gent.

THE FRIENDSHIP BOOK

Thursday — *June 12*

IT was heavy rain and I arrived home soaking. "These puddles are dreadful," I complained, but the Lady of the House was unsympathetic.

"Have you forgotten that talk we heard about the droughts in Africa?" she said. "People there would give anything to see all that wonderful water. Think how lucky we are!"

Needless to say, she heard no more complaints about my wet feet.

Friday — *June 13*

DURING the Depression of the 1930s, the New York Public Library was an invaluable resource for many who went to study there in an effort to improve their education and their prospects. Outside, two magnificent marble lions have guarded the main entrance since the impressive building was completed in 1911.

Known at first as Leo Astor and Leo Lennox, after the library's founders, they were later nicknamed Lord Astor and Lady Lennox, although they are both male.

When Fiorella Henry La Guardia was elected Mayor of New York in 1933, in the middle of the Depression, he renamed the lions Patience and Fortitude to encourage New Yorkers, as these were the qualities he felt they would need to survive.

Today, as Patience sits to the south and Fortitude to the north of the library entrance, these lions attract visitors from all over the world. They are a strong, visual reminder of the qualities needed to face up to and triumph over adversity.

Saturday — *June 14*

*M*ARIGOLDS *and butterflies*
And birds with tinted wings,
Are found in Nature's treasure box
Of many-splendoured things.
Snowdrops fairylike and frail
Which nod on slender stems,
Cartwheels of the spider webs
With frost-encrusted gems.

Red poppies 'midst the golden corn
The pansy's velvet face,
The starry curtain of the sky
Hung out in time and space.
Nature works with unseen hand
With artistry and skill,
Upon this living tapestry
Her purpose to fulfil.
Kathleen Gillum.

Sunday — *June 15*

AND Paul dwelt two whole years in his own hired house, and received all that came in unto him. Preaching the kingdom of God, and teaching those things which concern the Lord Jesus Christ, with all confidence, no man forbidding him.

Acts 28:30-31

Monday — *June 16*

BOBBY JONES, the famous American golfer, is the source of today's thought: "Friends are a man's priceless treasures, and a life rich in friendship is full indeed."

Tuesday — **June 17**

JOHN Howard Payne must have been quite a man. Who?, you'll probably say. Well, he was an actor in the first half of the nineteenth century and wrote a play called, "Clari, The Maid Of Milan".

Perhaps this still doesn't ring a bell with you, so what did this man do that was so memorable? Well, he wrote about something people the world over will agree with:

Mid pleasures and palaces though we may roam,
Be it ever so humble, there's no place like home.

Wednesday — **June 18**

CHARITY shops — we take them for granted these days. But to Svetlana, visiting Scotland from northern Bulgaria, they were something new, a way, perhaps, to help some of the poorest folk in her home region.

In an area that is so impoverished most things are re-used until they are past repair and charity shops are unheard of, Svetlana had to start with only the smallest crumbs from a poor society's table. But she took as her inspiration the Sermon on the Mount where, after Jesus had fed the gathered crowds with only five loaves and two fishes, the remaining crumbs filled twelve whole baskets.

A year later Svetlana's shop was so successful that she opened a second one. And what did she call the shops? Twelve Full Baskets.

It seems the feeding of the five thousand still goes on.

Thursday — **June 19**

DO you have a favourite Thinking Place? You may not actually call it by that name, but I suspect most of us have somewhere we like to go whenever life seems a little too complicated.

Our friend Bert finds that a walk in the hills often helps to clear his mind, the Lady of the House prefers pottering in the garden, while our neighbour Jonathan says that a day by the sea is the best way to get problems into perspective.

"I once read," he told us, "that Charles Morgan the novelist, described the sea as 'God's thoughts spread out' — and I know exactly what he means."

What a wonderful picture it paints. I do hope, wherever your Thinking Place happens to be, you find it just as inspiring.

Friday — **June 20**

THE BLESSING OF CREATION

*O CHRIST, there is no plant on the ground
But is full of your virtue.
There is no life on the land
But is full of your blessing.
There is no fish in the sea,
There is no creature in the ocean,
There is nothing in the heavens
But proclaims your goodness.
There is no bird on the wing,
There is no star in the sky,
There is nothing beneath the sun
But proclaims your goodness.*

Elizabeth Sutherland.

Saturday — **June 21**

A TEENAGE friend of young Hayley's was saying how boring her history classes were. "Why do we need to study the past? Surely the present and the future are all that matter," she mumbled.

The modern historian, A. L. Rowse, claims that the main purpose of history is to "enable you to understand better than any other discipline, the public events, affairs and trends of your time . . . History is about human society, its story and how it has come to be what it is."

In other words, it is only by studying the past that we can gain insight into the present and, in turn, gain guidance for the future.

Sunday — **June 22**

T RULY my soul waiteth upon God: from him cometh my salvation. Psalms 62:1

Monday — **June 23**

S IR James Young Simpson, the pioneer of anaesthetics, was once asked, "What has been your greatest discovery?"

He might have been expected to answer "Chloroform", for he was the first to use it to alleviate pain in childbirth. But instead this devout Scot replied, "The greatest discovery I ever made was that I was a lost, guilty sinner."

It was the faith he had found as a young man which inspired and drove his life's work in the service of others.

LOST TO THE WORLD

Tuesday — *June 24*

I WONDER if you've ever heard of the Darjeeling and Himalayan Railway? If you happen to be a steam train enthusiast then I'm sure you will, for it's a stunning example of late nineteenth-century engineering — a narrow gauge railway which puffs its way from the plains of West Bengal all the fifty-one miles and seven thousand feet up to Darjeeling.

Our friend Tony was lucky enough to visit it and came back full of admiration not only for the vision and faith of the original builders, but also for those who manage to keep it running today, over a century later.

"They have a sign by the workshop entrance," he told us, "which reads *Work Is Worship* — and no-one can deny that their craftsmanship works miracles!"

Wednesday — *June 25*

DESCRIBED as a lover of justice and lifelong supporter of the oppressed, the eighteenth-century clergyman, writer and wit, Rev. Sydney Smith said:

"When you rise in the morning make a resolution to make the day happier for a fellow creature. It is easily done — a leftover garment to a man who needs it, a kind word to the sorrowful, a little encouragement to the striving. Trifles? But look at the result.

"Even if you make only one person happy each day, this is three hundred and sixty five a year, if you live forty years you'll have made fourteen thousand people happy, at least for a while!"

Thursday — *June 26*

WHEN cartoonist Walter Lantz and his wife, Grace, rented a log cabin in a Californian forest for their honeymoon, their peace was shattered by an incessant tap-tapping on the roof. On investigation they discovered a woodpecker doing what woodpeckers do best.

Instead of letting the constant noise irritate them, Grace and Walter viewed the situation with good humour, and out of the experience the well-loved cartoon character Woody Woodpecker was born. Walter drew Woody, and later Grace provided his inimitable voice.

That pesky woodpecker turned out to be one of the best things that happened to them, Grace said later, but how different it would have been if they'd allowed themselves to be upset by it.

So often our approach to a situation is the most important thing, not the situation itself.

Friday — *June 27*

THOSE of us who have travelled in Tibet and the Far East might have been greeted by "Namaste".

For those of us who aren't so widely travelled, "Namaste" means "Hello", it means "Goodbye" and it means "I salute you". A useful word, all in all. And I know another translation: "The beauty in me sees the beauty in you."

This reminds us that everyone has this quality in them, some more obviously than others. Rest assured, though, it is always there, somewhere, just waiting to meet the beauty in you.

Saturday — June 28

ALBERT Einstein said, "There are only two ways to live your life. One is as though nothing is a miracle. The other is as though everything is a miracle."

From the moment we get up in the morning until we close our eyes at night, we are witnesses to miracles. Sprinkled throughout each day, we'll find them if we take time to look — a sunrise, birds singing, an encouraging word spoken at just the right time or perhaps a piece of music that inspires.

Wherever you go, keep an eye open for miracles. They paint life with glorious colours and are all around us, waiting to be noticed!

Sunday — June 29

AND the multitude of them that believed were of one heart and of one soul.   Acts 4:32

Monday — June 30

OUR friend Sean attends a flourishing youth group, and their meetings are never dull. He was telling me about a lively discussion which had taken place as each person tried to define the difference between hope and faith.

Happily, he said, one of the group had been able to come up with a quote from George Iles, which seemed to satisfy everyone: *Hope is faith holding out its hand in the dark.*

Yes, I like that idea too — don't you?

UNDER CYPRUS
SKIES

July

ISOBEL owns a gardening shop in a small town. She sells plants, bulbs, garden ornaments, and other items and gifts aimed at the green fingered.

She has a notice board in front of her shop where she likes to post inspirational sayings. One day she shared this thought:

Gardening is a way of showing you believe in tomorrow.

JONI Eareckson Tada has been quadriplegic since a diving accident in 1967 and her life has been spent in a series of wheelchairs. But rather than complaining about misfortune, she travels the world, showing people in difficult situations that life is still very much for living.

Joni compares her life to broken glass she found at home one day:

"I discovered that when the sunlight struck the shattered glass, brilliant, colourful rays scattered everywhere. That doesn't happen with plain glass. Your life may be shattered by sorrow, pain, or sin, but God has in mind a kaleidoscope through which his light can shine more brilliantly."

Thursday — **July 3**

"**B**EFORE we pass round the collection plate," a clergyman told his Sunday morning flock. "I'd like to share with you some old and wise words I once heard many years ago in a country church":

If ought thou hast to give or lend
This ancient parish church befriend,
If poor but still in spirit willing
Out with thy purse and give a shilling.
But if its depths should be profound
Think of thy God and give a pound.
Look not for a record to be given,
You'll get a receipt when you get to heaven.
The collection was a little larger that morning.

Friday — **July 4**

THE name Mary Isabella Beeton might not be instantly recognisable, but many thousands of homes were run along the lines described in "Mrs Beeton's Book Of Household Management". She was born in 1836 and her world was different from ours in so many ways, but her advice still stands today.

Leave nothing dirty; clean and clear as you go.
A good cook wastes nothing.
An hour lost in the morning has to be run after all day.
Haste without hurry saves worry, fuss and flurry.
Without cleanliness and punctuality good cooking is impossible.

These are rules which can be applied to many things in life.

Saturday — *July 5*

I'D stopped for a chat with James while he worked in his garden. After a while I made to leave.

"Wait," he said, starting to cut me a bunch of sweet peas. "Take some of these with you. I know the Lady of the House likes them."

"Leave some for yourself," I replied as he cut dozens of stems.

"Don't worry," he laughed. "I'll still have plenty left. You see, the more you cut sweet peas the more they grow."

I accepted his gift gratefully. I'd never realised it before but it seems that sweet peas have a lot in common with love — the more you give away, the more you have.

Sunday — *July 6*

AND he said unto me, Son of man, stand upon thy feet, and I will speak unto thee.

Ezekiel 2:1

Monday — *July 7*

I HAVE admiration for men such as Lord Nuffield and Andrew Carnegie who amassed great fortunes but believed their money to be worthless if it wasn't spent helping others. Indeed Carnegie said "the man who dies rich dies disgraced."

Not all of us get to build vast fortunes, of course. So what can you do if you're not a millionaire? I'd like to offer you this anonymous quote: "The greatest waste one can leave behind in life is the love that has not been given."

Tuesday — **July 8**

AN electrician was having an especially irritating day at work. A flat battery had made him over an hour late reaching my friend Andrew's business, his power tools were faulty and later when he wanted to go home, his van refused to start — again. So Andrew drove him home.

Andrew looked on, slighty puzzled as the electrician walked up the path towards his house, paused briefly beside a miniature tree and touched the tips of all the branches with both hands.

Sensing Andrew's curiosity the electrician turned and explained, "Oh, that's my Trouble Tree. I know I can't help having problems at work but they have no place at home so I hang them up on my tree each evening. Then in the morning I can pick them up again.

"Do you know," he continued, "there often aren't as many problems there as I thought."

Wednesday — **July 9**

IN my Summer times of happiness
Remind me, Lord, You're there,
And let me build up trust in You,
Your steadfast love and care.
Then, when the troubled Winter times
Come crowding round my door,
I'll find my faith is strong and true
And I have hope in store.
Through all the seasons of my life,
Whatever time may bring,
Lord, lead me always on with You
Towards eternal Spring.

Iris Hesselden.

Thursday — *July 10*

TERRY Waite was at the peak of his career. As special envoy to the Archbishop of Canterbury he travelled the world and met heads of state. When he first began to work for the release of Western hostages in the Middle East, he gave a go-between a Prayer Book to pass to the hostages, hoping it might bring them some comfort.

Then his world turned upside down when he himself was taken hostage. The next three years were to be spent in solitary confinement.

With no-one to talk to and nothing to occupy his mind, he craved something to read and something to help him keep track of passing time. Imagine his astonishment when one of his jailers handed him a well-read prayer book. It had words of comfort and a theological calendar and it was, in fact, the same book he had sent out three years before!

Terry Waite had no idea when he sought to comfort a distressed soul that he would, one day, be helping himself as well.

Friday — *July 11*

ONCE, when Jim was a young man, he was up against an obstacle to all his hopes and plans. He saw no way of overcoming it until a friend, an older man, said, "Look at it as if it was a rock. You can either let it block your way or you can use it as a stepping stone."

As soon as he said this Jim was determined to overcome adversity — and he did.

Saturday — *July 12*

THERE'S a story I like about William Murdoch, the Scotsman who invented gas lighting. Down on his luck and almost penniless, he applied for a job with James Watt's engineering company.

The interview wasn't going too well. A nervous Murdoch dropped his hat from his lap and it fell with an unexpected thud. It seems he didn't own a decent hat to wear to his interview, so he shaped one from wood on a home-made lathe and painted it to look the part.

Some folk, when they're laid low, give up. Others find new reserves of determination and try something that might never have been done before. His prospective employer could see which sort Murdoch was. He was offered the job and went on to make our world a brighter place.

Sunday — *July 13*

FROM that time Jesus began to preach, and to say, Repent: for the kingdom of heaven is at hand.   Matthew 4:17

Monday — *July 14*

MOST of us would agree with the idea that our souls are of greater importance than our bodies, yet a lot of the time our spirits are starved because we tend to think of them so little. We need to water our spirits like plants, make sure that they don't shrivel and die.

Just a few minutes of soul time each day can make all the difference.

Tuesday — *July 15*

DO you know the story behind St Swithin's Day? Swithin was Bishop of Winchester in the ninth century. He was well loved so his last wish was granted when he was buried outside the West Door of the Old Minster.

A century later, on 15th July, 971, his bones were dug up and reburied inside the Cathedral. As if in protest the heavens opened and it was claimed that it rained for forty days.

St Swithin has never been forgotten and every 15th July people still look at the sky and hope it won't rain, just in case . . .

Wednesday — *July 16*

THE Lady of the House and I discovered a second-hand bookshop, one which neither of us had visited before. We spent a long time happily browsing, but it wasn't until later that the Lady of the House observed that she sometimes felt books were just like people.

"There are those with attention-grabbing covers, but which on closer acquaintance often disappoint; there are classics which no longer surprise, but are always good to meet again — and then there are the modest-looking volumes which tend to get tucked behind others, but can reveal themselves to be real gems in disguise."

I laughed. "So which category would you put me in?"

She thought for a moment. "Definitely an old favourite."

That's good enough for me!

Thursday — *July 17*

*SOMETIMES you just need an angel
To stay by your side through the day,
Sometimes you just need an angel
To help you, and show you the way.
An angel to shield you and watch you,
To lend you endurance and grace
To stand by your side and to guide you
When life seems a worrying place.
But courage! — for angels are with us,
Just waiting to love us and care.
Just trust, and you'll find when you need one,
An angel will always be there.*

Margaret Ingall.

Friday — *July 18*

A VISION without a task is a dream. A task without a vision is drudgery. But the two together are the hope of the world.

Saturday — *July 19*

DAILY SURVIVAL KIT

Toothpick — to remind you to pick out the best qualities in others.

Rubber Band — to remind you to be flexible.

Pen — to remind you to list your blessings every day.

Tube Of Glue — to remind you to stick with it; you can accomplish that task.

Tea Bag — to remind you to relax daily.

Bandage and Plasters — to remind you to heal hurt feelings, yours and someone else's.

Sunday — **July 20**

INASMUCH as ye have done it unto one of the least of these my brethren, ye have done it unto me.
Matthew 25:40

Monday — **July 21**

ARE you feeling disheartened? Has life been getting you down or has it taken an unexpectedly difficult and challenging turn? Well, then, these words may help to give you a fresh perspective:

Find the flower in yourself and give it the chance to bloom.

Tuesday — **July 22**

GILLIAN loves her new hobby — she collects images of sunsets and is known to her friends as "the Sunset Girl".

"I keep them in my photo album and in a special file on my computer," she says. "They are photographs taken by friends in different countries who never miss an opportunity to catch glowing images of the sun going down in different parts of the world."

The American writer Joseph J. Mazzella believes "Every sunset is different and yet each one is so beautiful. Each is full of fantastic colours, from radiant reds, to glorious greens, to peaceful purples, to outstanding oranges, to breathtaking yellows."

There is endless joy and a sense of peace when watching the sun set, whether over the mountains, the oceans or even the deserts.

Wednesday — **July 23**

ROBERT Louis Stevenson did not enjoy the best of health but still managed to leave his mark on the world. Perhaps these words give us some idea of the man's spirit.

"Even if the doctor does not give you a year, even if he hesitates about a month, make one brave push and see what can be accomplished in a week."

An inspirational quote whatever the state of your health.

Thursday — **July 24**

HERE are some wise words by the Persian poet Kahlil Gibran: "Old age is the snow of the earth; it must through light and truth give warmth to the seeds below, protecting them and fulfilling their purpose."

Friday — **July 25**

AS you step out to enjoy the warmth of the sun on your skin, the smell of new-mown grass, the vibrant colours of the countryside and wispy clouds in an azure sky, remember, you don't have to be just a spectator. You, too, can play your part in the glory of a Summer's day.

The poet Joseph Addison wrote:
What sunshine is to flowers
Smiles are to humanity.

So spread a little sunshine and brighten someone's day.

Saturday — *July 26*

I WONDER if you have ever heard of Alfred and Bentley Ackley? The two brothers were born in America in the 1880s, and grew up to become a talented team of hymn writers. When young, they received their musical training from their father, but later attended the Royal Academy of Music in London. The hymns they wrote are many and varied, but I would like to share with you today some words from "He Will Not Let Me Fall".

When grief is more than I can bear,
Too weak am I to call,
If I but lift my heart in prayer.
He will not let me fall.

Words of faith to give courage to all of us.

Sunday — *July 27*

AND he informed me, and talked with me, and said, O Daniel, I am now come forth to give thee skill and understanding.　　　　Daniel 9:22

Monday — *July 28*

I MUST use each precious moment
For it may not come again,
And I can never be content
With things that might have been.

Good words I fail to say this day
May ever be unsaid,
For I may not get the chance again
On the winding path ahead.

　　　　　　　　　　Anon.

Tuesday — *July 29*

THE Greek philosopher, Euclid, once inadvertently offended his brother. Completely forgetting the ties of family, the latter was consumed with rage and his irritation boiled over.

"May I die if I am not revenged upon you at one time or another!" he shouted.

Euclid responded, "And let me die if I do not soften you by my kindness and make you love me as well as ever."

Wednesday — *July 30*

AS I prepare for bed at night
Keep me in Your care,
And hear my grateful thanks, O God,
In this simple prayer.

For all the blessings of the day,
For family and friends,
For safety as the night draws near
And the daylight ends.

And when the night has passed away
And sunlight paints the dawn,
Please, God, wake me in grateful mood
To greet the coming morn.
                              Ann Rutherford.

Thursday — *July 31*

"MAKE a career of humanity and you will make a greater person of yourself, a greater nation of your country and a finer world to live in."
                              Martin Luther King Jr.

August

Friday — **August 1**

WE'VE been away for two whole weeks
   Just me and mine together,
The rain poured down, our feet got wet,
   But who cared about the weather?
We shared the chores in our caravan
   Played board games by the hour,
And each time that we braved the storms
   We were caught in another shower.
And yet those days of simpler life
   They taught us all so much
That what we have is here and now
   When loved ones stay in touch.

Jenny Chaplin.

Saturday — **August 2**

WHEN the "Lord Of The Rings" films were released, they were praised for their special effects. But author J. R. R. Tolkien had a spiritual side to his writing and these words, spoken by Gandalf, warm my heart — and, I hope, yours — with their promise of a better future:

"Other evils there are that may come . . . Yet it is not our part to muster all the tides, but to do what is in us for the succour of those years wherein we are set, uprooting the evil in the fields that we know, so that those who live after may have clean earth to till."

COTSWOLD CORNER

Sunday — *August 3*

SING, O heavens; and be joyful, O earth; and break forth into singing, O mountains: for the Lord hath comforted his people, and will have mercy upon his afflicted.   Isaiah 49:13

Monday — *August 4*

TODAY I want to write in praise of knees. They may not all be beautiful but think how useful they are! When there is a weed to be dug out, often the only way is to get down on our knees.

While out walking you may well catch sight of an unusual plant — you will see it best on your knees. You have dropped some small item — you will have to search on your knees.

Above all, people of many faiths sink to their knees in worship and prayer, the ultimate act of humility and love. God bless and protect our knees!

Tuesday — *August 5*

OUR old friend Mary looked out across her garden and said, "Isn't it wonderful, Francis, that flowers should remind us of good friends?"

I agreed, and I couldn't resist giving a reminder of two apt thoughts about the link between flowers and friends:

Friendship, like flowers, blooms ever more fair,
  When carefully tended by friends who care.
Life is a garden, good friends are the flowers,
And times spent together are our
  happiest hours.

Wednesday — *August 6*

A HUNDRED and forty years ago Edward Hale wrote a short story entitled, "Ten Times One Is Ten". In it ten strangers gather for the funeral of Harry Wadsworth, only to discover that he had helped each of them in a time of need.

In memory of their old friend they each resolve to do the same for ten other needy folk. If each of those hundred folk did the same, then Harry Wadsworth's legacy of benevolence would encircle the globe in no time . . .

Fans of the story set up a charitable organisation called the Lend A Hand Society — and they are still doing good works today. Each of us could be a Harry Wadsworth, or we might have been helped by someone like him, so why not pass a good deed on? In the words of the author of that original story:

Look up and not down,
Look forward and not back,
Look out and not in —
Lend a hand!

Thursday — *August 7*

M ANY people nowadays spend a lot of time tracing their family tree. It has become a popular hobby among all age groups. I was amused to hear this tongue-in-cheek description of it:

"Genealogy is something you take up when you realise you don't know where you are going — but at least you can find out where you've been!"

Friday — *August 8*

THEY are in many respects both curious and remarkable animals, intelligent, quaint and affectionate. You would probably never guess that the writer of these words was speaking about tortoises!

He was Sir Peter Eade, the greatly-loved physician at the Norfolk and Norwich Hospital from 1858-1888. In that time he oversaw huge improvements for patients, pioneering new treatments and earning great affection and respect.

He was elected Mayor of Norwich, made a Freeman, and had a road named after him.

After a long day Eade liked nothing better than to go home and relax in the company of his tortoises — this great public figure was a simple man at heart.

Saturday — *August 9*

"MEMORIES of our lives, of our works and our deeds will continue in others." So said Rosa Parks. She was the black woman who refused to move to the back of the bus she was travelling on and sparked the boycott that later led to the repeal of the United States' discriminatory race laws.

It isn't given to most of us to be in the right place at the right time to make our mark on history but by, for example, showing guidance to a child, helping someone in need and living a life as best as we can, we can still leave an impression on the hearts of those we meet which will be remembered long after us.

BEAUTY SPOT

Sunday — *August 10*

AND God called the light Day, and the darkness he called Night. And the evening and the morning were the first day.   Genesis 1:5

Monday — *August 11*

TWO people went on the same package holiday. One came back complaining about the weather, the hotels and the food. "It was terrible," he grumbled.

The other said, however, that he had loved it. "We saw such interesting places, and met such friendly people. I learned so much."

Well, maybe everything wasn't perfect. But I know which of the two I would rather go on holiday with — not the one who picked fault all the time, but the one who made the best of it and gained from the experience.

Tuesday — *August 12*

IT'S a little disrespectful, I know, but some people speak about "wrinklies" when talking about older folk.

Well, there is nothing wrong with a few wrinkles. Some of the most beautiful faces I have seen have been covered in them. It's a mistake to try to cover them up for they tell of a long and often interesting life.

I have heard them described as "Nature's tracery" while Charles Dickens who had a few himself in later years, said that every wrinkle is "but a notch in the quiet calendar of a well-spent life".

Wednesday — **August 13**

DURING the Second World War a popular comedian, Tommy Trinder, brightened life for thousands of Londoners by putting up billboard placards saying, "If It's Laughter You're After, Trinder's The Name."

Making people laugh in difficult times has been an invaluable tonic to so many. As Erma Bombeck says: "If you can laugh at it, you can live with it."

Thursday — **August 14**

EACH time you think that Life's unfair,
Because the burden's hard to bear;
Or when you feel inclined to sigh
That fame and fortune pass you by —
Think of those, who have no sight,
And live their days in endless night;
Think of those, who cannot hear
The voice of Spring, so soft and clear;
Think of those, who have no voice
To speak with others and rejoice;
Think of those, who lie and pray
For strength that they may walk some day;
Think of each unhappy life
Shattered by both grief and strife;
And cast aside the mournful view,
That life brings nought but care for you;
For surely they are more inclined
To say that life has been unkind
Think of them, and then recall
You're not unlucky after all.
                              John M. Robertson.

Friday — *August 15*

GREEN-fingered readers will understand the great gardener Percy Thrower's memorable words: "Despite all the attractions of the world of publicity and entertainment my heart still stayed — and always will stay — in the garden and among the plants I love."

Saturday — *August 16*

I WAS touched by the story of Florence Martus. As a young woman she lived in Savannah, Georgia, where there's now a bronze statue of her on the riverfront. What did she do to deserve this honour? She waved at strangers.

Florence's brother was the quarantine officer on an island in the Savannah River. Ships entering the estuary would signal information about the health of their crew before docking.

Florence lived with her brother and took up the habit of waving to every ship that sailed past. She waved a handkerchief in the daytime and held a lamp at night. Sailors from all over the world came to expect and look forward to a friendly welcome as they passed by.

How many lives could we brighten today, how many lonely folk could we reach out to, with a wave, a friendly, "How are you?"

Sunday — *August 17*

AND were beyond measure astonished, saying, He hath done all things well: he maketh both the deaf to hear, and the dumb to speak. Mark 7:37

Monday — *August 18*

COULDN'T the world be arranged so that everyone was happy all the time? Why must it be the way it is with its many ups and downs?

Well, the evangelist Billy Graham had this to say: "Out of pain and problems have come the sweetest songs and most gripping stories."

The poet Robert Hamilton wrote:

I walked a mile with sorrow
And ne'er a word said she
But, oh, the things I learned
When sorrow walked with me.

Just know there is a reason. We might not understand it now — but we will.

Tuesday — *August 19*

THESE lines were seen by a reader in her favourite magazine and they are well worth passing on:

One song can tell a story,
One wish can wake a dream,
One seed can start a forest,
One bird can herald Spring.

One hand begins a chain of love,
One candle lights a room,
One love can bring a spark of hope,
One hope can conquer gloom.

One voice can speak with courage,
One heart can know what's true,
One life can make a difference —
One life belongs to you!

Wednesday — *August 20*

DARREN, about to start college, was showing his father the long reading list he'd been given. "It's a lot to tackle," he admitted, "but as our history teacher always said, when it comes to doing any task there are always three choices.

"We can either 'give up, give in, or give it our all'. So I've decided to choose the latter," Darren said.

His teacher sounds a wise person and somehow, I don't doubt that Darren will follow in his footsteps!

Thursday — *August 21*

MADELEINE Carroll, born in West Bromwich, became one of Hollywood's most glamorous stars of the 1930s. The world was at her feet, but after the death of her sister in a 1940 bombing raid on London she turned her back on glamour to work as a Red Cross nurse in France and Italy. Later, she helped concentration camp victims to come to terms with their ordeals.

She returned to acting from time to time but only when her work for others allowed. Many of those she supported had no idea who she was or what she had given up to be there for them.

Friday — *August 22*

WHAT lies behind and and what lies before us are small matters compared to what lies within us. Ralph Waldo Emerson.

Saturday — *August 23*

I LIKE these words by Scotsman Thomas Carlyle, the famous writer and philosopher, who was born in 1795 in Ecclefechan.

"There is no life of a man, faithfully recorded, but is an heroic poem of its sort rhymed or unrhymed."

His words are a tribute to us all, for they recognise that life presents challenges to take up, obstacles to overcome, the unexpected which we must come to terms with, while never forgetting that life also gives many blessings for us to rejoice in.

Sunday — *August 24*

A ND it came to pass, that, as they went in the way, a certain man said unto him, Lord, I will follow thee whithersoever thou goest.

Luke 9:57

Monday — *August 25*

Y OU can search throughout the entire universe for someone who is more deserving of your love and affection than you are yourself, and that person is not to be found anywhere. You yourself, as much as anybody in the entire universe, deserve your love and affection. Buddha.

In other words, if you don't love yourself, you cannot love others. When you love others as you love yourself, you will do to them as you would like them, in turn, to do to you.

Tuesday — *August 26*

SPENDING a day or two with her feet up after twisting an ankle, our friend Sheila was delighted by the number of friends who "just happened" to drop by. She found that when she was on her own she thought about her discomfort, but when in company she thought only about her friends. All pain was forgotten.

The monk, Aelred of Rievaulx, summed it up nicely some nine hundred years ago when he said, "No medicine is more valuable, none more suited to the cure of all our ills than a friend we may turn to in time of trouble and with whom we might share our happiness in time of joy."

Wednesday — *August 27*

LORD who made the vales and mountains,
Bush and shrub, each tiny flower,
Worked your art on crystal fountains,
Kindly sent us sun and shower;
May the season's bright creations
Spread the meaning of your power,
While the glowing constellations
Light the nightly, velvet hour,
Then, as we awake to morning,
Give us strength to face each day:
Filled with wonder, at the dawning
Of new hope, in hearts to stay.
Elizabeth Gozney.

Thursday — *August 28*

ANGER is the only thing to put off until tomorrow. Czech Proverb.

GOING
FISHING

Friday — August 29

WHAT do you have in common with a President of the United States? Not much, you might say. But I can think of two things. First, there's the way you deal with the trials each day sends.

Harry S. Truman described his day like this: "I come to the office each morning and stay for long hours doing what has to be done to the best of my ability. And when you've done the best you can, you can't do any better."

Secondly, you have the knowledge that no matter how great or weak your power there is always Someone else you can rely on.

"So when I go to sleep," President Truman continued, "I turn everything over to the Lord and forget it."

Saturday — August 30

AMY was in an antique shop when she saw a small Victorian embroidery in a frame decorated with mother-of-pearl. Looking closely at it, she read these words:

Fear knocked on the door. Faith answered. And lo, no-one was there.

Amy bought the attractive handicraft as a birthday present for a friend's collection. These wise words give us all much to think about.

Sunday — August 31

THOU art Peter, and upon this rock I will build my church.   Matthew 16:18

September

Monday — *September 1*

MAHATMA Gandhi is widely revered as the founder of modern India.

He found inspiration in both Islam and Christianity, especially the Sermon on the Mount, as well as his native Hinduism. He studied law in London, and practised for twenty years in South Africa before returning to India.

One day, as he stepped on board a train, one of his shoes slipped off and landed on the track. He could not retrieve it because the train was already on the move.

To his companions' surprise, Gandhi calmly took off his other shoe and threw it back along the track to land close to the first. When asked why he did this, he smiled and replied, "The poor man who finds the shoe will now have a pair that he can use."

Tuesday — *September 2*

TRY to take a few moments today to think about these anonymous words — I hope you'll agree that they contain a wealth of truth.

Love is like playing the piano. First you must learn to play by the rules, then you must forget the rules and play from your heart.

Wednesday — *September 3*

WHAT are you waiting for? A change in the weather? Fewer family commitments? The chances are that by the time these things change, there will be some other reason for not doing that good turn.

Let's remember the advice of Anne Frank, the young Jewish girl who perished in the Holocaust.

"How wonderful it is," she wrote, "that nobody need wait a single moment before starting to improve the world."

Thursday — *September 4*

THE spirited Fanny Crosby was known as the "Hymn Queen" in New York. Blinded at the age of six weeks, during her long life she wrote over 9,000 poems and hymns before her death in 1915 at the age of 95.

Yet in many ways Fanny is best remembered for the optimism she possessed all her life, and the tireless work she did to help others. Her first poem, written at the age of eight, is evidence of her happy nature and positive outlook on life:

Oh what a happy soul am I
Although I cannot see,
I am resolved that in this world
Contented I will be.

At that early age, Fanny had realised that the decision to be content and make the most of every circumstance, was hers to make. Life may not always be easy, but we are at least free to choose the way we live it.

REFLECTIONS

Friday — **September 5**

"MY Uncle Stan," Donald said, "was the most wonderful kite-maker. We always loved visiting him because we knew that not only would he help us make and fly our own kites, but as long as we tried our best he wouldn't be cross if they weren't quite perfect."

I like the sound of Uncle Stan. Sometimes it's easy to become so obsessed with attaining perfection that anything less loses all value for us. I go along with a remark made by the actor Michael J. Fox, who said, "I am careful not to confuse excellence with perfection. Excellence I can reach for; perfection is God's business."

Saturday — **September 6**

A SHIP that never sailed the seas
　Or foundered in a stiffened breeze,
Never by the helm been steered,
　　Gone adrift and disappeared,
Doesn't seem to be much use,
　　At least that's what one could deduce,
But this special ship is rare,
　　The sort that only two can share
And pull together as tho' one,
　　Steadfast till each day is done,
To last and last right to the end,
　　Because, you see, her name is "Friend"!
　　　　　　　　　　　Brian H. Gent.

Sunday — **September 7**

THEN laid they their hands on them, and they received the Holy Ghost.　　Acts 8:17

Monday — **September 8**

ELIZABETH Fry was a young woman who pioneered prison reform. One of her first missions was to alleviate the condition of women being deported in chains to Botany Bay. In an effort to calm a hysterical girl, Elizabeth pressed upon her a Bible, some scraps of fabric, some thread, needles and tea.

The day after Elizabeth died, a letter was delivered to her home from an Australian mother. It explained how she had arrived as a convict, turned her life around and had been happily married for twenty years. The quilt that had covered the woman's bed was made from scraps pressed upon her by "an Angel of Mercy".

Elizabeth never judged the convicts she worked amongst. "The good principle which beats in the hearts of many abandoned persons may be compared to the sparks of a nearly extinguished fire. By means of the utmost care and most gentle treatment they may yet be fanned into a flame."

Tuesday — **September 9**

IT was Fred's eightieth birthday. Most of the folk on his street, young and old alike, attended his celebrations.

Later Fred told me his secret: "I once came across a comment from the silver screen actor Frederic March, who said: 'Keep interested in others; keep interested in the wide and wonderful world. Then, in a spiritual sense you will always be young.' And that," said Fred, "exactly sums up my own philosophy!"

Wednesday — **September 10**

ISAAC was a nervous child. Born in Trowbridge, Wiltshire, in 1813, he fainted so often in the noisy classroom that he had to leave school aged twelve.

However, he was eager to learn and though he took a factory job he studied at home before and after work. By the time he was eighteen years old he was able to go to London for teacher training.

He became fascinated with shorthand and devised a completely new system. It caught on and students flocked to the Institute of Phonetics he opened in Bath.

By the time Sir Isaac Pitman died, aged eighty-four, he knew that Pitman's Shorthand was recognised as the best method for rapid note-taking. Despite all the advances in technology it is still used today.

Thursday — **September 11**

I'M sure when William Feather, the American author and publisher, wrote these words he wanted to make his readers think deeply.

"Something that has puzzled me all my life," he wrote, "Is why, when I am in special need of help the good deed is usually done by someone on whom I have no claim."

Well, of course, there is no apparent reason for such selfless acts, unless we see those unexpected helpers as brothers and sisters, acting under the direction of a loving Father. Then what other claim would we need?

Friday — **September 12**

L ARRY is a lecturer at a large college in town. He's worked there for many years and, due to his infinite reserves of patience, is a favourite among both colleagues and students.

A friend once asked him how he managed to keep so calm, and received Larry's smiling explanation that he always did his best to bear in mind the words of philosopher Ludwig Wittgenstein, who said: "If people never did silly things, nothing intelligent would ever get done."

What a cheering and encouraging philosophy — and one worth remembering next time we start to feel impatient with the fallibility of others — and ourselves!

Saturday — **September 13**

L OOKING back from our twenty-first century perspective, the civilisations of the ancient Greeks and Romans seem far away. However, while daily life has changed enormously, some things remain very much the same.

For example, Marcus Cicero, a Roman High Consul, had this to say on friendship: "Friends are close to one another even when they are apart, they are rich even when they are poor, ready to help even when ill. It seems impossible, but they are alive even when they have passed away."

Friends have always been the same.

Sunday — **September 14**

F OR as many as are led by the Spirit of God, they are the sons of God.   Romans 8:14

Monday — *September 15*

AS I was sitting in our little book-room with its cosy carpet, the walls bright with firelight, I thought of these lines by the writer and poet Andrew Lang, who spent his life in the world of the printed word:

One gift the Fairies gave me
The love of books, the Golden Key
That opens the Enchanted Door.

I am sure many of you love books — old ones, new ones, each presenting a world rich in fact or fiction. I think of them all as good companions — books are a window on the world, one which we can open at any time.

Tuesday — *September 16*

TODAY the sun was blazing bright,
The sky a perfect blue,
And all among the garden plants
I worked the whole day through.
The heavy air was hushed and hot,
With not a breath of breeze,
The only movement, butterflies,
And pollen-drowsy bees.
But sleepy hours have come and gone
And slowly dulled the sky,
A hazy cloud hides the sun,
And thunder rumbles nigh.
It's time to go inside and watch
The storm-clouds have their way,
I know tomorrow morn I'll find
A bright, new shining day.
Margaret Ingall.

Wednesday — **September 17**

O CHRIST Jesus,
  When all is darkness
And we feel our weakness and helplessness,
Give us the sense of Your presence,
Your love, and Your strength.
Help us to have perfect trust
In Your protecting love
And strengthening power,
So that nothing may frighten or worry us,
For, living close to You,
We shall see Your hand,
Your purpose, Your will through all things.

St. Ignatius of Loyola.

Thursday — **September 18**

IT'S odd, isn't it, how misfortune can affect us all in different ways. When Daniel's business failed, it seemed for a while that the blow had cut so deep he might never entirely recover.

Then gradually, and with the support of those closest to him, he began to look around for other options, eventually turning his life around to the point where he now acts as a counsellor for others caught up in the same situation.

"It took me a while to realise," he said, "that I could actually build upon my misfortune, and use it for good. In fact," he added, "my inspiration came from some words of an American, Robert H. Schuller, who said, 'Let your hopes, not your hurts, shape your future'."

Brave and wise words which all of us can build upon.

Friday — **September 19**

I'M sure we've all heard of the medical condition "a hole in the heart". Tony Anthony's condition was just as serious. Let me explain.

Sent from Britain to China as a child he found himself excluded by the local children. When he returned years later he found himself a stranger, even to his own parents, so to combat bullying Tony took up Kung-Fu, eventually becoming World Champion. His life seemed on the up, until his fiancée died in a car crash.

A job as a bodyguard allowed him to vent his frustrations through his martial arts but eventually, he went too far and ended up desperate and alone in a Cyprus jail cell.

It was there that a missionary, Michael Wright, diagnosed Tony's problem. He had a God-shaped hole in his soul! It's a common complaint and some folk try to fill it with drink, drugs or violence. Tony had tried these. They didn't work. So he tried something different — Jesus.

Now Tony is an author, travelling the world, promoting a message of peace and faith. He's happier than ever and all because he found the right way to fill the hole in his heart.

Saturday — **September 20**

ONE of William Wordsworth's most famous poems is "Daffodils", but he loved all flowers. For him, even the smallest and most modest were part of Nature's great plan.

As he put it in one poem:
The daisy, by the shadow that it casts,
Protects the lingering dewdrop from the sun.

GOOD
NEWS

Sunday — *September 21*

ARISE, go unto Nineveh, that great city, and preach unto it the preaching that I bid thee.

Jonah 3:2

Monday — *September 22*

WELCOME the harvest, the season of plenty,
  Rejoice in the gifts of the fruit and the grain
And celebrate nature, she gives of her bounty,
  Bestowing sunshine and warm, Summer rain.
The earth and the ocean, the river and sky,
  The beauty and wonder abound everywhere,
The crops in the field and the trees in the forest,
  The joy of creation for each man to share.
So welcome the harvest, reach out to each
  other,
  And lift up your voices in praise and in song,
Go forward together, remember your brother,
  And share a new harvest-time all the year long!

Iris Hesselden.

Tuesday — *September 23*

"YOU know," observed our friend Maureen, "I was dreading the building of all that new housing, but how wrong I was! Fresh faces add so much to the community."

Maureen hadn't been alone in her concern about how her village would cope with its new inhabitants, so it was good to hear that fears were proving unfounded. Many of us find the thought of big changes and new faces rather daunting, but we're often pleasantly surprised when the time comes.

Wednesday — *September 24*

"I'VE been reading children's tales," announced the Lady of the House as she returned from visiting a neighbour. "Rosie's two little girls asked for a story, so I read them one about a young princess who, even though she lived in a palace of gold, was still unhappy because she didn't have any friends."

"I hope it had a happy ending," I said.

"Oh, yes," she replied. "But do you know, it also made me think of some words which Joyce Grenfell wrote: 'Friendship is the most precious privilege that this earthly experience can offer.' Don't you think that's true?"

I do indeed — and fortunately, though it may be more precious, it's also a lot easier to acquire than a golden palace!

Thursday — *September 25*

IT'S hard to believe but in the Old South of America peanuts were considered a useless crop, grown only for the good they did the soil. George Washington Carver, known as The Plant Doctor, despaired of them.

"Mr Creator," he is quoted as saying. "Why did you make the peanut?"

Eventually Mr Carver devised over 300 marketable uses for the nut, including peanut butter, which he gave away rather than patent.

I'm not a peanut expert and I only know a little about George Washington Carver, but I'm sure of one thing — he turned to the right person for advice!

Friday — September 26

A PRIMARY school teacher stopped to speak to one of his pupils who was standing by himself in the playground looking dejected.

"Jamie, why is today the best day of your life?"

The young lad looked puzzled. "I don't know, sir. It doesn't feel like it."

"Ah, but I'm right, Jamie. Think about it. You have never been taller than you are today. You have never been stronger than you are today. You have never been wiser than you are today. So congratulations to you!"

Jamie grinned. As he ran off to join his companions, he suddenly felt taller and stronger and wiser, and that felt good.

Saturday — September 27

W E don't seem to hear the old proverbs so often nowadays. A pity, because they contain so much good sense and some of our greatest men and women have lived by them.

Winston Churchill said anyone who never went to college could make up for it by reading the proverbs.

Alexander Graham Bell described proverbs as the shortest road to wisdom, while Lord Byron said that, in proverbs, "a drop of ink makes thousands think".

Let's not forget them!

Sunday — September 28

I T is God that girdeth me with strength, and maketh my way perfect.   Psalms 18:32

Monday — *September 29*

WHAT use are gorse bushes when you want to plant a garden? In 1834 social reformer Augustus Smith found that the islands of Scilly were scoured by winds that seemed to blow all the way from America. His dream of planting a garden to be proud of seemed doomed before he started.

Walking out over his land Smith would dip into pockets full of gorse seeds and scatter them — these hardy plants can survive in the harshest of conditions. In their shelter he planted larger bushes.

Today, exotic trees and plants from all over the globe grow in his Abbey Gardens, often referred to as "Kew with the roof off".

Augustus Smith didn't waste any time worrying about what he couldn't do — with those tiny gorse seeds he found the only thing he could do and built his dream on that.

Tuesday — *September 30*

THE Lady of the House and I visited a photographic exhibition taking place in a village hall. We admired several studies of the Cairngorms looking at their most majestic.

"They must have seen such a lot of history," I commented. "If only they could speak . . ."

The Lady of the House smiled and drew my attention to a small notice underneath which quoted a poet called Linda Hogan:

There is a way that Nature speaks. Most of the time we are simply not patient enough, quiet enough to pay attention to the story.

October

CYNTHIA and Ella went for a drive in the countryside. Ella wanted to take her friend on an outing that would lift her spirits.

Autumn was everywhere — brilliant orange, russet, red, and copper clothed the trees and tinged the forests. As they drove through a hilly part of the countryside, they stopped to view a valley spread out below.

"Oh," exclaimed Cynthia, "What a masterpiece! I'm so glad that God shares His beauty with us."

Her faith and appreciation for life's natural gifts had made her approach the day with gratitude — something we should all do, every day!

SIR Humphry Davy, the Professor of Chemistry at the Royal Institute in London who invented the Davy Safety Lamp to protect miners from explosions of firedamp, also wrote words of wisdom with which to lighten the lives of others. Judge for yourself:

"Life is made up, not of duties or great sacrifices, but of little things, in which smiles, kindness and small obligations given habitually, are what preserve the heart and secure comfort."

Friday — *October 3*

"WHEN nothing is sure, anything is possible." The well-known writer Margaret Drabble made this comment in connection with writing fiction.

It certainly describes the blank page or computer screen confronting a writer, who may stare at it in uncertainty for hours but finally creates a whole world out of the multitude of possibilities it offers.

These words are just as relevant to other aspects of life, too. When the future looks unclear and we can't see what lies ahead, it is easy to be discouraged. If there are too many complicated decisions to be made it is tempting to do nothing.

But if we think for a moment we can see that uncertainties, in fact, present us with a wealth of possibilities. We can then, like an author, begin to aim for a story with a happy ending.

Saturday — *October 4*

TODAY is the feast day of St Francis of Assisi. He believed in preaching outdoors, so he would often address his sermons to the sky and the trees and the creatures in the field.

Once he addressed the birds in the trees by saying, "Good morning, theologians." When asked why he explained that many people who classed themselves as such spent all their time deep in study, in dimly-lit rooms, cut off from the world.

Then he pointed to the birds and said, "Only those creatures who truly understood God's love could spend the whole day singing."

Sunday — *October 5*

NOW the Lord of peace himself give you peace always by all means. The Lord be with you all.   Thessalonians II 3:16

Monday — *October 6*

BRENDA is friendly with Daphne-next-door, and over the years they have shared many a cheerful chat and many a pot of tea. She was smiling broadly when she showed me this rhyme, written by her neighbour, which shows why they have enjoyed such a lasting rapport:

We share the daily crossword
We share a daily brew,
I share my garden's bounty,
You share your home-made stew.
We know each other's welcome
To all upon our shelves
But here's our pact — with head-colds
We keep them to ourselves!

Tuesday — *October 7*

TEN THINGS TO KEEP IN MIND

YOUR presence is a present to the world;
Count your blessings, not your troubles;
Decisions are too important to leave to chance;
Nothing wastes more energy than worrying;
Try not to take life too seriously;
Friendship is a wise investment;
Life's treasures are people working together;
Do ordinary things in an extraordinary way;
Make time to reflect and wish upon a star;
Take the days just one at a time.

Wednesday — *October 8*

HAVE you ever noticed how gardens reflect the seasons? What could be more appropriate, in early Spring, than the pure white snowdrops? As the weather becomes warmer, they are followed by yellow daffodils, a taste of brighter colours to come.

Bluebells mirror the skies of early Summer and, as the sun grows warmer, we feast our eyes on the reds, pinks and oranges of high Summer with its roses.

In time they give way to the softer, more mellow hues of chrysanthemums until, with the year itself, they fade and die.

The wonderful thing is that this pageant of the garden will all happen again next year.

Thursday — *October 9*

THIS prayer, which was often recited in air-raid shelters during the days and nights of the Blitz during the Second World War, is no less relevant today:

Increase, O God, the spirit of neighbourliness among us,
That in peril we may uphold one another,
In calamity serve one another,
In suffering tend one another
And in homeliness and loneliness
In exile befriend one another.
Grant us brave and enduring hearts
That we may strengthen one another,
Till the disciplines and testing of these days
be ended.

Friday — **October 10**

IN the 1960s, singer and songwriter Pete Seeger took some much-loved words from the Biblical book of Ecclesiastes and adapted them to go with the haunting music he had written. The result was a massive hit, and an enduring song that has remained popular over the decades:

To everything there is a season and a time for every purpose, under heaven.

Yet while things come and go, there are also special times for different people in our lives. Some are there for a specific reason at a specific time, perhaps in times of trouble, and then they move on as troubles pass. Some are there for a season. It may be that we make special friendships when our children are small, but as they grow the ties loosen.

Others, like family, are with us for a lifetime and are probably the most important people of all. While we take care to cherish the friends who come in and out of our lives, let's not take for granted those who are with us all of the time.

Saturday — **October 11**

TAKE the threads of life and weave them
Blending hope and joy and love,
Take the sunshine and the shadows
And the starlight from above.
Weave the colours of the seasons
And the dreams within your heart,
See the picture always growing
Every day another start.

Iris Hesselden.

Sunday — *October 12*

JESUS said unto him, Thou shalt love the Lord thy God with all thy heart, and with all thy soul, and with all thy mind.   Matthew 22:37

Monday — *October 13*

SOMEONE once told me, "There are no boring days, only boring people." I knew what he meant for in a world as full of wonder as this, it almost requires a special effort to be bored, but this phrase always seemed such a harsh way of putting it.

Then I read some words by President Roosevelt's wife, Eleanor, saying the same thing but, I think, in a much more inspiring way.

"One thing life taught me," she wrote, "If you are interested, you never have to look for new interests. They come to you."

Tuesday — *October 14*

IF we make quiet space
  Where we can draw apart,
To seek God's hidden strength which lies
  Deep down within the heart,
To sense His calming presence
  Which seeps into the soul,
Refreshing and renewing
  And seeking to make whole —
We'll find respite from worldly cares
  A great release it brings,
When we take time to meditate
  Upon eternal things.
                              Kathleen Gillum.

Wednesday — **October 15**

"FLOWER Drum Song" might not be the best known of the Rogers and Hammerstein musicals, but it does contain one of my favourite songs. In "A Hundred Million Miracles" the cast recount just a few of the amazing things that happen every day, from the changing of the weather, the hatching of an egg, to the fact that, even after all these millions of years, the sun still rises in the morning.

Now a hundred million miracles might be a bit much to expect you to collect, even on a lovely sunny day, but five or six shouldn't be too hard to find. And you'll notice, I'm sure, that each one you spot will make your load lighter and your mood brighter.

Thursday — **October 16**

FOR those of us who might be feeling a little less than in the full flush of youth, here's how Sir Walter Scott described "the middle life":

"Reaching the other side of the hill has its drawbacks. The wind is not so good, the limbs are not so tireless as in the ascent; the stride is shortened and, since we are descending, we must be careful in placing our feet.

"But on the upward road the view was blocked by the slopes and there was no far prospect to be had except by looking backwards. Now the course is mercifully adapted to failing legs, we can rest and reflect, since the summit has been passed and there is a wide country before us, though the horizon is mist and shadow."

Friday — *October 17*

I LOVE seeing images of the Arctic and Antarctic. The icebergs with their luminous colours are unique, quite breathtaking, but everyone knows that the part we see above the water is nothing compared to what lies below.

Likewise, the grand cathedrals which have stood the test of time throughout the centuries also reach great depths. Their foundations reach far below the ground and, along with the cornerstone, they are of vital importance to the stability of the building. In the nineteenth century a church tower in Wales came crashing to the ground just after it was completed, and all because of a faulty cornerstone.

This is a lesson we can apply to our lives. We may have dreams and hopes for the future, but without the foundation of hard work and the cornerstone of commitment, these will amount to nothing. As Henry David Thoreau said:

"If you have built castles in the air, your work need not be lost; that is where they should be. Now put the foundations under them."

Saturday — *October 18*

THOSE who wish to sing always find a song.
Swedish Proverb.

Sunday — *October 19*

BUT now, O Lord, thou art our father; we are the clay, and thou our potter; and we all are the work of thy hand.   Isaiah 64:8

Monday — **October 20**

IT'S strange, isn't it, how despite all our advances in knowledge, some things about human nature never change. Take our capacity for worrying, for example.

As long ago as the third century Marcus Aurelius Antoninus, Emperor of Rome, wrote: "Never let the future disturb you. You will meet it, if you have to, with the same weapons of reason which today arm you against the present." It's wise and comforting advice which is just as valid today.

And if that fails to cheer, it might be worth remembering another saying, this time from Niels Bohr, who wrote: "Prediction is very difficult, especially about the future."

Tuesday — **October 21**

IT'S funny, isn't it, how some people seem to cope with criticism, but if you pay them a compliment they don't know how to accept it.

Our friend May was a little like that. Whenever her friends exclaimed with delight over her light-as-air cakes, she would blush awkwardly. Happily, as time has gone by, she has become much more gracious about receiving praise due, she confided, to some words she read by Eleanor Hamilton:

"A compliment is a gift, not to be thrown away carelessly, unless you want to hurt the giver."

"It made me realise," May admitted, "that other people like to give as well as receive — and presents can come in many forms, whether cakes or compliments!"

Wednesday — *October 22*

THERE is a tall, slim tree at the bottom of our old friend Mary's garden, and one day she watched it toss and sway in a strong breeze. Yet no matter how far the branches moved, the bottom of the trunk stood firm, as its roots dug deep into the ground.

It occurred to her then that often when something comes to challenge us, we are tempted to struggle against it. Perhaps instead we should stand with our feet steady, like the tree's strong roots, yet be prepared to give a little, too. Sometimes pushing against something or somebody will achieve nothing.

As she looked out at that tree the next day, it stood upright and still. The storm had passed, and the tree was still standing tall. If it hadn't moved, it would have snapped.

Thursday — *October 23*

SAD to say, there will be times in almost all our lives when we feel we have reached the end of our tether and just can't go on. I don't know who wrote these simple yet profound words on the subject but they are well worth passing on.

"Take a deep breath. If you can hold on one moment longer, and then one moment more, you'll find that the moments become seconds, the seconds add up to minutes and the minutes become hours, until you've held on long enough to catch your second wind. Then, with careful confidence, climb upwards until you reach the top."

Friday — **October 24**

OUR friend Joanne, who cheerfully admits to being somewhat short-sighted, was laughing as she recounted an incident one morning.

"I bent down to pick up what I thought was a piece of paper from the floor, only to find it was a square of sunlight coming through the window! But wouldn't it be nice if we could pick up a patch of sunlight, and put it in our pocket for later?"

It would indeed. However, though we cannot literally do this, there's nothing to stop us trying to keep some sunshine in our hearts. After all, who knows how many cloudy days it might brighten!

Saturday — **October 25**

FOR most of us losing our hearing would be a tragedy. How much more acute would that loss be for someone whose life was dedicated to music?

At the age of twenty-eight Ludwig van Beethoven's hearing began to deteriorate and he realised that he would become completely deaf. Did he rage against this? Did he curse the injustice of it all? No.

He said, "I will submit to all changes and I will put my whole confidence, O God, only in Thy unchangeable goodness."

His most inspirational works were yet to come.

Sunday — **October 26**

FOR there is one God, and one mediator between God and men, the man Christ Jesus.

Timothy I 2:5

Monday — **October 27**

ONE of the most awe-inspiring sights in Autumn is that of geese flying in formation, as they play follow-the-leader and spread out behind that lone first bird in a V-shape.

It is interesting to learn why they do this. As each bird flaps its wings, the uplift assists the bird following immediately behind. It's reckoned that the flock can fly over seventy per cent farther by helping each other along this way.

Should one bird fall away from the rest, it quickly discovers how much harder it is to fly alone and rejoins the others. When it gets tired the leading bird will drop back and another will take its place. The following geese will honk to encourage those upfront to keep up speed.

If only we would work together more, encourage one another and share a common purpose like the geese, just think how much more we could achieve.

Tuesday — **October 28**

THE Lady of the House and I agree with these words by the poet Robert Southey:

"No distance of place or lapse of time can lessen the friendship of those who are thoroughly persuaded of each other's worth."

Robert, born in Bristol in 1774, and later made Poet-Laureate in 1813, lived for the last forty years of his life at Greta Hall near Keswick in the Lake District. There, although his means were very modest, he provided a home for some time for the family of his friend and brother-in-law the poet Samuel Taylor Coleridge.

Wednesday — *October 29*

ELBERT Hubbard was born into a poor family in 1856. His first job was selling soap door-to-door; he retired, aged thirty-five, a rich man.

Nobody's fool, you might think. But he himself would have disagreed with that as reflected in his words which give us all a little leeway.

"Everyone is a fool for at least five minutes every day; wisdom consists in not exceeding the limit."

Thursday — *October 30*

I'VE heard it said that life is ten per cent what happens to us and ninety per cent how we respond to it. Every morning we are given a new day to unwrap; it's what we do with the gift that determines our tomorrow.

Friday — *October 31*

I BELIEVE that Love is meant and of eternal significance. I believe that Beauty is meant and of eternal significance. I believe that Goodness is meant and of eternal significance.

I believe that Life itself, and especially that wonderful spark of creative life that runs through us each day, is meant and of eternal significance.

There is a God and that God is the source of all true love, beauty, goodness and imagination. God calls to us through Jesus not to despair for these things are eternal and, insofar as our lives are bound up with these eternal things, we shall find eternity too.

Elizabeth Sutherland.

November

*P*EOPLE are so funny,
I'm sure you will agree,
They do so many silly things —
They're not a bit like me!
I see the funny things they drink
The awful things they eat,
I'm really much more choosy,
(Those cream buns look a treat!)

They spend so much, collect so much
To fill their house or flat,
I just collect small teddy bears,
There's nothing wrong with that!
I see the funny clothes they wear,
Short shorts and plastic boots,
And men in sporty training shoes
With navy business suits.

From six feet tall to five feet small
I watch the things they do,
And every day I'm glad to say
That I'm not funny too!
                    Iris Hesselden.

*A*ND, Thou, Lord, in the beginning hast laid the
foundation of the earth; and the heavens are
the works of thine hands.   *Hebrews 1:10*

Monday — *November 3*

I WONDER if you know the story of the lily leaf, said to have helped to inspire the design of a visionary building which gave pleasure to many people.

The building was Sir Joseph Paxton's Crystal Palace, built in London's Hyde Park to house the Great Exhibition of 1851. The leaf was that of the South American white and rose lily *Victoria regia* named after the young Queen Victoria.

This river lily's leaves were of an impressive size with a three or four-inch edge. But it was their network of veining which, along with the great conservatory Paxton had designed at Chatsworth, helped to inspire his great, glittering Crystal Palace of glass and iron.

In 1854 the Crystal Palace was moved to Sydenham in London where, surrounded by parkland and gardens, it hosted numerous events and continued to give pleasure for years.

Flowers and their foliage are a great inspiration. As a Persian proverb says: "The world is a rose; smell it and pass it to your friends."

Tuesday — *November 4*

WHILE reading about British missionaries' work in China during the early part of the twentieth century, our old friend Mary came across a motto that was popular then.

"Oh, Lord," it went. "Convert the world — and begin with me!"

It's a reminder that we all should strive to make our lives an everyday message of goodness.

Wednesday — **November 5**

L ES NICHOL was the last in a long line of Galloway shepherds. He lived and worked on the Scottish Border hills all his days, tending to his flocks. Les once spoke of lambing time.

"It was fine if you were 'in by' and had a shed to take the ewe to overnight, but if you were out on the hills the shepherd just had to turn his collar up and pull his cap down and spend the night with the sheep."

Didn't you get bored, he was asked. Les scoffed at the very idea. It would be a poor man, he insisted, who didn't have enough in his head to think about for a night or two.

"And if ever I ran out of things to talk to myself about," said Les, "well, that's when I listened while the Lord did the talking."

The greatest Shepherd of all eventually called Les home. One cared for humble sheep, the other cares for humble humans. I'm sure they have a lot to talk about.

Thursday — **November 6**

O N one of these stormy Winter evenings best spent by the fireside I read a few lines by the poet Thomas Hood which made me think:

The Summer never shines so bright
As thought of in a Winter's night.

A perfect description of the impact of a Summer's day; even the thought of one can brighten the darkest and dreariest of Winter evenings. The anticipation of a sunny day has the power to warm many a downcast heart.

FIRM
FOOTING

Friday — **November 7**

GARY was collecting his paper when I walked into the newsagent's.

"You know," he said, as he glanced down at the headlines, "All these rich and famous people often seem to have more problems than anything else."

It's certainly not a new idea that money doesn't guarantee happiness, but Gary's words made me think of Albert Schweitzer, who took it even further: ". . . one thing I know, the only ones among you who will be really happy are those who have sought and have found how to serve".

Saturday — **November 8**

CATCHING THE LIGHT

SOMETIMES it's about running to stand
In sunlight splayed through the forest;
To drink upwards the light, pure
Until you are filled. But you know
  as well as I do
There are days it is dark always;
You wander hopeless through storms of
  branches, lost,
Weary for rest. Yet this is faith —
  Not burying the little light that is left
Inside, but firing the heart onwards
  To the morning that lies hidden
Under the whole of the hills.
                    Kenneth C. Steven.

Sunday — **November 9**

AND to you who are troubled rest with us, when the Lord Jesus shall be revealed from heaven with his mighty angels.   Thessalonians II 1:7

Monday — **November 10**

THE Lady of the House has a fine selection of sugared almonds on display in a cabinet. However, they're not for eating — they were "favours" given out at weddings.

I had no idea what the real significance of these little laced and beribboned treats was until our old friend Mary explained.

They started off as an Italian tradition, it seems. The almonds are bitter, but the candied shells are sweet and they represent the good times and the not-so-good times a couple might come across as they made a life together. The ribbons tied around them represent the devotion that holds everything in place.

And to think I once thought they were just sweets!

Tuesday — **November 11**

THE eleventh of November
A special time of year
No roses bloom, nor daffodils
  Yet red poppies all appear.

Such frail and dainty little flowers
  And yet how proud they stand
As they say a silent thank-you
  In every corner of the land.

The eleventh of November
  An emotive time of year
When the courageous little poppies
  Salute those who cast out fear.
                    Jenny Chaplin.

Wednesday — **November 12**

AFTER a forest fire, the rangers began their journey to assess the damage. One ranger found a bird perched on the ground at the base of a tree — dead and completely covered in ashes.

However, when he investigated further, three tiny chicks emerged from beneath their mother's wings. She had carried her offspring to safety at the foot of the tree, realising that toxic smoke rises. She could have flown to safety but chose to shelter her chicks, sacrificing her life so that they could live.

"He will cover you with His feathers. Under His wings you will take refuge."   Psalms 91:4

Remember the One who cares about you, and then be different because of it.

Thursday — **November 13**

OUR friend Hannah bought her young grandson an inflated balloon. It was in the shape of Pooh Bear with a big smile on his face.

Paul was intrigued and loved the way it floated upwards. However, after about a week Hannah and her family noticed that Pooh wasn't quite so plump any more; the air was escaping.

Gradually, as the days passed, poor Pooh became more and more deflated until he was reduced to a flat, floppy piece of plastic.

"What a shame," said Hannah. "But never mind — at least he's still smiling!"

If only we could be like that balloon. When we get deflated by life's ups and downs we should always try to remain positive in our outlook.

Friday — **November 14**

OUR old friend Anon. presents us with these wise words today:

It is not what we eat
But what we digest
That makes us strong;
Not what we gain
But what we save
That makes us rich;
Not what we read
But what we remember
That makes us learned;
And not what we profess
But what we practise
That gives us Integrity.

Saturday — **November 15**

SURELY there is always a way to make any day worthwhile. As Harry Fosdick wrote:

"Life seldom gives a man a day so barren that chances to help someone are not plentiful; to appreciate some fine, unadvertised endeavour of an unnoticed man; to speak a stout word for a good cause; to be kind to the humiliated and gracious to the hurt; to touch some youth with new confidence in human kindness and fresh resolve to live for noble ends — such opportunities are as free as the air to breathe."

Sunday — **November 16**

NOW set your heart and your soul to seek the Lord your God; arise therefore, and build ye the sanctuary of the Lord God.   Chronicles I 22:19

KEEP US
SAFE

Monday — **November 17**

MAKING someone happy can be the work of a moment but according to Sidney Smith the effects can be felt through decades.

"Mankind is always happier for having been happy," he wrote. "So that if you make them happy now you make them happy twenty years hence — by the memory of it."

Tuesday — **November 18**

IT was a copy of Robert Burns' poems, bought from a Scots pedlar with a fine singing voice, which led American John Greenleaf Whittier (1807-92) to try his own hand at poetry. He'd started life as a farm boy and later became a maker of slippers, but it was only after his sister had sent some of his verses to a newspaper that his career as a writer began.

He was from a Quaker family who had fled from England to avoid persecution and perhaps this background gave the impetus to his campaign to abolish slavery in the United States.

His mode of dress and style of speech were always that of a Quaker, but he maintained that two hundred years of silence had taken all the "sing" out of their members. "I know nothing of music," he said. "A good hymn is the best use to which poetry can be devoted, but I do not claim that I've succeeded in composing one."

Modest words indeed from a man who left us with, amongst many other compositions, one which begins with the familiar words: "Dear Lord and Father of mankind, forgive our foolish ways."

Wednesday — **November 19**

A HUNDRED and fifty years ago Lydia Child wrote these thought-provoking words:

"The cure for all the ills and wrongs, the cares, the sorrows, and the crimes of humanity, all lie in the one word. Love. It is the divine vitality that everywhere produces and restores life."

Thursday — **November 20**

I LOOKED upon a Winter world
And whispered, "Are you there?"
And for a second, so it seemed,
*   My plea met empty air.*
And then, though nothing outward changed,
*   I felt a change in me,*
As though a gentle voice had asked,
*   "Dear child, oh, can't you see?*
I'm here in every blade of grass,
*   In every plant that grows,*
I'm in the sun, the clouds, the sky,
*   In every breeze that blows.*
I live in every bird and beast,
*   In every human face,*
I am the shining cord that binds
*   Each colour, creed and race."*
And as I heard the voice, I felt
*   A comfort deep inside,*
A shining, sweet assurance
*   That no doubts could override.*
The question I had dared to voice
*   With yet no hope of balm,*
Had brought me peace beyond compare,
*   And filled my heart with calm.*
                    Margaret Ingall.

Friday — *November 21*

THERE are things we can choose to do — or not do — but growing older isn't one of them. Day by day it happens to all of us, though we can still choose the manner in which we age.

That's why I was delighted when the Lady of the House shared with me this verse by Mrs Karle Wilson Baker:

Let me grow lovely growing old —
  So many fine things do.
Laces and ivory and gold
  And silks need not be new.
And there is a healing in old trees;
  Old streets a glamour hold;
Why may not I, as well as these,
  Grow lovely, growing old?

Saturday — *November 22*

AS a young man trying to make his way in the world, Matt suffered one setback after another. He told me, "I was ready to give up."

Then a good friend gave him a lesson. "You see this rubber ball," he said, and he threw it to the ground, first softly, then harder. "The harder it's thrown down, the higher it bounces back. That's how you have to approach life."

A simple thought, but it made all the difference to Matt's thinking, and to his life.

Sunday — *November 23*

AND they entered into a covenant to see the Lord God of their fathers with all their heart and with all their soul.   Chronicles II 15:12

Monday — **November 24**

RON took a leisurely walk into the country, relaxing and forgetting the rush and bustle of trying to get through a supermarket queue or waiting for green at the traffic lights. It was a delight just to have time to "smell the daisies" and admire the scenery, he told me later.

I was reminded of these words of advice from the prolific thinker Ralph Waldo Emerson: "Try to adopt the pace of nature; her secret is patience." It's the right pace to adopt, I'm sure, in what some have called "an age of impatience".

The Italians have a centuries'-old proverb that puts it well: "He who has no patience has nothing at all." Meanwhile the Dutch have a saying: "An ounce of patience is worth a pound of brains."

Tuesday — **November 25**

EDDIE has always loved sport, and at one time had hopes of making it his career, until a serious accident put paid to his plans.

"And yet in a way, the long convalescence did me a favour," he said. "It gave me time to take stock of my life and look around me, rather than just focusing on the single goal I'd been aiming for. It allowed me to understand that I could find just as much happiness and fulfilment by enjoying the things that I could still do."

His words reminded me of a comment made by the writer Ursula K. Le Guin: "It is good to have an end to journey toward; but it is the journey that matters in the end."

Make sure you enjoy it!

Wednesday — **November 26**

HAVE you ever had visitors ring your doorbell when you're vacuuming in your slippers or when your grandchildren are there, making it look as if you live in a toy factory?

A little embarrassing? Well, not if your visitors are familiar faces. You may live in the humblest of homes but a friend stepping over the threshold will make it a special place.

With this in mind I'd like to share with you a blessing for visitors from the Inuit people:

The lands around my house are more beautiful
From the day when it is given me to see
Faces I have not seen for long.
All is more beautiful and life is thankfulness.
These guests of mine make my house grand.

Thursday — **November 27**

I CAME across Thomas Jefferson's ten rules for the good life, each worth its weight in gold:

Never put off till tomorrow what you can do today.
Never trouble another for what you can do
   yourself.
Never spend your money before you have it.
Never buy what you do not want because it is
   cheap; it will never be dear to you.
Pride costs us more than hunger, thirst, and cold.
Never repent of having eaten too little.
Nothing is troublesome that we do willingly.
Don't let the evils which have never happened cost
   you pain.
Always take things by their smooth handle.
When angry, count to ten before you speak;
   if very angry, count to one hundred.

Friday — **November 28**

OUR friend Enid was telling me how much she depends on the word hope.

"Hope means so much on bad days when things go wrong," she said. "Hope is the element that inspires us to try — and try again. Hope is what encourages us to keep on living, learning and loving.

"Hope will never abandon us when life is unexpectedly filled with things which sadden and disappoint. Hope will get us through the truly rough times."

Saturday — **November 29**

IT was Karen's birthday, and her friends had dropped in to wish her many happy returns.

"I must admit," she said, "I was feeling a bit gloomy when the day began. The years seem to fly by so quickly, and I wasn't sure I was ready for yet another birthday. Then there was a ring at the door which made me realise how silly I was being, for the postman had arrived with a whole bundle of cards and gifts.

"From now on, I've decided that I shall regard my birthday not as a sign of how old I'm becoming — just as a wonderful reminder of how rich in friends I am."

Now that's the sort of treasure that is always worth accumulating!

Sunday — **November 30**

AND as soon as he had spoken, immediately the leprosy departed from him, and he was cleansed.
                                                    Mark 1:42

December

HERE is a story from Hindu folklore. One day, a man saw a scorpion struggling in a deep pool of water. He decided to try to save it by stretching out a finger but the creature instantly stung him. Again, the man tried to remove the scorpion from the water but he was stung again.

An onlooker urged him to give up and go home. But the would-be rescuer said: "It is the nature of the scorpion to sting. It is my nature to love. Why should I give up my nature because it is contrary to the way of the scorpion?"

BORN into a poor Scottish family in 1848, Mary Slessor went out to work as a missionary in Calabar. At her own request she lived with a tribe in a remote part of the jungle.

She had a city upbringing, first in Aberdeen, then Dundee, and had once been too afraid to cross a field of cows. Now she had to walk, often alone, through dense bush infested with lions.

"Many a time," she wrote, "I walked along praying, 'O, God of Daniel, shut their mouths', and He did!"

Wednesday — **December 3**

ST FRANCIS de Sales wrote these words in the 16th century and they still, I believe, have relevance for us today:

Do not look forward in fear to the changes
*   in life;*
Rather look to them with full hope that
*   as they arise,*
God, whose very own you are, will lead you
*   safely through all things;*
And when you cannot stand it, God will
*   carry you in His arms.*
Do not fear what may happen tomorrow;
The same everlasting Father who cares for you
*   today will take care of you every day.*
He will either shield you from suffering or will
*   give you unfailing strength to bear it.*
Be at peace and put aside all anxious thoughts
*   and imaginings.*

Thursday — **December 4**

JUNE has an interesting way of keeping her cool. We all know the technique of counting to ten before speaking when something rubs us up the wrong way.

Well, instead of muttering "One, two, three," and so on, she slowly recites to herself the words, "Our, Father, Who, Art . . ."

The first line of the Lord's Prayer has exactly ten words and, by the time she has recited them, June usually remembers that her "problem" is part of a bigger plan and is already being taken care of by Someone much more patient and understanding.

Friday — **December 5**

CONNIE used to be a lively member of a chorus line that graced the old variety shows. Today she lives quietly, and still keeps in touch with some of those she danced beside in the theatres of the 1950s.

One evening, feeling a little low, Connie was thinking back to life as it was then. Suddenly, these words came to mind, first read in a book of quotations:

Whenever a cloud appears in the blue,
Remember, somewhere, the sun is shining —
So the best thing to do
Is to make it shine for you!

Saturday — **December 6**

THE feast day of Saint Nicholas who later became famous worldwide as Santa Claus is 6th December. Born to wealthy parents, Nicholas was orphaned as a child. He became a Christian and proceeded to give away his entire fortune to people in need — mostly children.

One tradition has him reaching into windows and dropping gold into the stockings which poor children had hung up to dry, not unlike a tradition many of us still follow! Isn't it reassuring to know that the man who started the legend of Santa Claus was true to the teachings of Jesus, and spent his life quietly doing good for others.

Sunday — **December 7**

VERILY, verily, I say unto you, If a man keep my saying, he shall never see death.

John 8:51

REACH FOR
THE SKY

Monday — *December 8*

OUR friend Patricia was reading about Sir Peter Ustinov, that much-missed actor, author and raconteur.

Though born in England, he came of Russian, German, French and Italian stock, and entertained audiences all over the world. In his later years he also became a Goodwill Ambassador for UNICEF, visiting needy children and using his talent to amuse as a means of raising funds.

"I was," he once said, "irrevocably betrothed to laughter, the sound of which has always seemed to me to be the most civilised music in the world."

Tuesday — *December 9*

IN his book "Miracle On The River Kwai" Ernest Gordon described the harrowing conditions and brutal treatment which his fellow prisoners-of-war suffered. However, in the midst of it all they had the heart to put on some shows for entertainment.

One that had made an impression was "The Dance Of The Scarecrow" in which a lone dancer played a scarecrow being buffeted by music representing the winds of misfortune:

I listened again to the conversation in front of me.

"Reminds you of Charlie Chaplin, doesn't he? He says to you that life is a knock-about but you've got to keep going. It's the keeping going that makes him human, isn't it? Whenever he stops a bit, or lies down — he's just a scarecrow. Ain't that right?"

It was then, and it still is.

Wednesday — **December 10**

ELEANOR has lived alone for years now, and although both her sons live abroad, I've never once heard a hint of self-pity in her voice.

"You see," she once told me, "much as I love my children, I knew it wouldn't be fair to expect to come first in their lives for ever. So I resolved never to slide into regarding myself as a second-class person — not in a selfish manner, I hope," she added quickly.

"But by being good to myself in little ways, such as treating myself to a new outfit, or perhaps the best seat at a concert. You see, I've always found that being kind to oneself is good practice for being kind to other people."

I can heartily endorse that philosophy. Be nice to yourself, for you are of value!

Thursday — **December 11**

STAR of Hope —
   Shine in the night of hunger and despair,
Bringing to those who cry for food and freedom
   News of the advent of the Lord of Hope.

Star of Peace —
   Shine in the warring darkness of men's minds
Spreading the light of kindness and compassion
   That marks the coming of the Prince of Peace.

Star of Love —
   Shine in the chilly depths of human hearts,
Kindling a warming glow of golden glory
   Around the cradle of the King of Love.
                                   S. G. Munro.

Friday — **December 12**

"THE great thing about getting older," wrote author Madeleine L'Engle, "is that you don't lose all the other ages you've been."

Well, Chinese tradition has it that we live our lives in twelve-year segments. After our first five "ages" — in other words, by the time we are sixty, we are reckoned to be physically and materially complete. Our responsibilities are mature enough to take care of themselves and we can devote ourselves to a little "soul gardening", cultivating our spiritual well-being.

Saturday — **December 13**

*I THOUGHT the time had come to bake
That rather special Christmas cake,
And so I started to prepare
  And weigh the fruit and flour with care.
I warmed the oven, greased the tin
  And felt a certain pride within.
It smelled so good in just a while,
  I thought it sure to raise a smile.
But later I was not amused —
  I found the eggs I should have used!
So, bakers, now this warning take,
  Be careful with that special cake!*
                                        Iris Hesselden.

Sunday — **December 14**

AND when he had gathered all the chief priests and scribes of the people together, he demanded of them where Christ should be born.
                                        Matthew 2:4

Monday — *December 15*

WILLIAM Hazlitt, the essayist, felt like any father would when he left his son at boarding school. Missing the lad before the gates were closed and worrying about how he would cope, he wrote the following advice:

"Always, my dear, believe things to be right until you find them the contrary; and even then, instead of irritating yourself against them, endeavour to put them right or put up with them the best you can. Never anticipate evils or make them out worse than they are. It is a good old rule to always hope for the best."

Many things have changed since then, but I find myself in complete agreement. Looking for the best is still a "good old rule".

Tuesday — *December 16*

THERE'S a story told of St Malo who had worked all day in the fields. Having finished his work he went to pick up his cloak and found that a wren had built her nest in it. Not only that, she had laid her eggs in the nest.

Remembering that God loves all his creatures and hears when the smallest bird falls to the ground, St Malo left his cloak where it was — and not just for the day. He left his cloak around the nest until the eggs hatched and the chicks learned to fly on their own.

"And this was the marvel, that all the time the cloak lay there, there fell no rain upon it."

This tale may only be a legend, but it reminds us that if we do all we can, God will take care of the rest.

Wednesday — **December 17**

SUGGEST to some people that they are blessed and they will look puzzled.

But one man who didn't need to be told of his good fortune was Steven Callaghan. While attempting a solo crossing of the Atlantic, his yacht sank. Scrambling into his dinghy he realised he was alone and miles from the shipping lanes, had little in the way of supplies and hadn't been able to send out an SOS.

He floated, lost, for fifty-nine days before his life-raft sprung a leak. For the next seven days and nights he tried desperately to pump more air in than was leaking out; he grew weaker all the time.

When fishermen found him he had survived longer than anyone ever had adrift on the ocean. But why hadn't he given up? What had kept him going?

"I kept telling myself," said Steven in his book, "that compared to what others had been through I was fortunate."

For him counting his blessings was more than just an old saying — it was a way of saving his life.

Thursday — **December 18**

PART of the wonder of the festive season is that it can be found in the smallest of things and in the humblest of people. I particularly like these lines by Eva Logue:

"A Christmas candle is a lovely thing; it makes no noise at all, but softly gives itself away."

Friday — **December 19**

A GREAT deal of beautiful and much-loved music is associated with Christmas. One such composition is Johann Sebastian Bach's Christmas Oratorio which was composed when the great master of organ music was choirmaster and organist at St Thomas's Church — the Thomaskirche — in the beautiful city of Leipzig where he lived for twenty-seven years.

Bach, who came from a musical family, was born in Eisenach in Thuringia in 1685 and died in Leipzig in 1750. He was a devoted family man, and his second wife Anna Magdalena, with whom he had thirteen children, collaborated with her husband. She copied out music and also took part in performances. Sadly, in later life Bach became blind.

Today Leipzig celebrates Bach's lasting achievements with a yearly Bach festival.

"Music exalts each joy, allays each grief . . . softens every pain," wrote the 18th-century physician and poet John Armstrong. Johann Sebastian Bach would surely have agreed.

Saturday — **December 20**

K EEP a green tree in your heart and perhaps a singing bird will come. Chinese Proverb.

Sunday — **December 21**

W HEN they had heard the king, they departed; and lo, the star, which they saw in the east, went before them, till it came and stood over where the young child was. Matthew 2:9

Monday — *December 22*

OUR old friend Mary received a greetings card with these memorable lines:

*I wish you enough sun to keep your
attitude bright;
I wish you enough rain to appreciate
the sun more;
I wish you enough happiness to keep
your spirit alive;
I wish you enough pain so that the smallest
joys in life appear bigger;
I wish you enough gain to satisfy your wanting;
I wish you enough loss to appreciate all
that you possess;
Finally, I wish you enough "Hellos" to sustain you
through to the final "Goodbye" .*

Tuesday — *December 23*

EMPEROR Constantine is credited with converting the Roman Empire to Christianity. Before that, though, as ruler of half the then known world, he had almost limitless power, and wasn't always immune to its corruptions.

Visiting Bethlehem, his mother, the Empress Helena, recalled the three Kings who brought gifts for Jesus. Though they were powerful men they were prepared to pay homage to a carpenter's son. They laid aside their pride for their Lord.

Reflecting on her son's problems she had but one prayer for him: "May he, too, before the end, find a kneeling place in the straw."

Riches won't do it. Power won't do it. But a humble heart and honest faith will see the greatest and the least of us safely home at last.

Wednesday — **December 24**

AT this time of year one of the world's favourite flowers is the beautiful bright poinsettia, and associated with this is the story of a miracle.

According to Mexican legend a poor girl was watching others taking gifts to a statue of baby Jesus. She began to cry for she had nothing to give.

An angel suddenly appeared and told her to gather weeds along the road, then offer them as her present. When she laid them beside the manger, they were instantly transformed into the brilliant poinsettia.

The flower is named after Dr Joel Poinsett, the first American ambassador to Mexico who, in 1828, fell in love with the beauty of the fiery red plant. Later, he took it to the United States.

Now, each December, poinsettias by the million adorn festive homes around the world.

Thursday — **December 25**

THERE are many different Christmas customs worldwide. In the Black Forest region of Germany there's something unusual about the family Christmas meal — an extra place is set at the table for the Virgin Mary. Not that anyone expects her to arrive in person; it's just a way of trying to make up for the time she was turned away from the inn.

This festive season, let's try to remember those who have been rejected or left out, and find a place in our hearts — or at our tables — for them.

Friday — **December 26**

SEVEN-YEAR-OLD Bobby was asked in a survey what "love" means. "Love is what's in the room with you at Christmas if you stop opening presents and listen," he said.

Let's put aside the "wisdom" of our years and listen for a moment like a child.

Saturday — **December 27**

IN 1927 a twenty-five-year-old Scot arrived in New York. With just enough money in his pocket to last him two weeks, he had no clear idea of where he was heading.

However, twenty years later Peter Marshall was living in the nation's capital as chaplain to the United States Senate, one of the most influential churchmen in the country.

Peter remained a humble, down-to-earth man whose eloquence, humour, dedication to his calling and zest for life ensured he was loved by all who knew him. He was just forty-six years old when he died, yet he used his time wisely, as befitted "a man of contagious spirit, eager and alert, quick to see opportunities of service and to meet their challenge . . . a builder of the kingdom of God on this earth".

As he himself said, "It's not the duration of a life that counts, but the donation."

Sunday — **December 28**

AND the glory of the Lord came into the house by the way of the gate whose prospect is toward the east.   Ezekiel 43:4

THE FRIENDSHIP BOOK

Monday — **December 29**

ARCHBISHOP Desmond Tutu is well known for his words of wisdom and the following are no exception: "Do your little bit of good where you are; it's those little bits of good put together that overwhelm the world."

Tuesday — **December 30**

*BE generous when giving praise
Express appreciation,
Uplifting and encouraging
    Without hesitation.
A word from you could be the spur
    That sends folk on their way,
And gives them hope to carry on
    And face another day.*
                    Kathleen Gillum.

Wednesday — **December 31**

TOAST TO THE FUTURE

*HERE'S to the old year and here's to the new,
Here's to visions and dreams coming true,
A world filled with harmony, peace for mankind,
With bounty for sharing and want hard to find.*

*A toast to the future, and all it can hold,
With moments to treasure and love to enfold,
With hope for tomorrow, dispelling all fears,
And faith growing stronger and warming
    the years.*

*Go forward with courage, no doubt or dismay,
The future is waiting, beginning today!*
                    Iris Hesselden.

Photograph Locations and Photographers

INSPIRATION — *Santiago de Compostela, Spain.*
FROSTY FRAME — *Back Walk, Stirling.*
CLOUDLESS DAY — *Chatsworth House, Derbyshire.*
ON THE RIGHT TRACK — *Glenfinnan Viaduct, Highlands.*
THE GREAT OUTDOORS — *Brantwood Gardens, near Coniston.*
CAPTURE THE MOMENT — *Glenashdale Falls, Arran.*
BIRDS OF A FEATHER — *Haddenham, Buckinghamshire.*
BLUE HORIZON — *Lulworth Cove, Dorset.*
COTSWOLD CORNER — *Quenington, Gloucestershire.*
BEAUTY SPOT — *Rydal Water, Lake District.*
GOING FISHING — *Connemara, Eire.*
REFLECTIONS — *Linlithgow Park and Loch.*
THE FALLS — *Wain Wath Force, Swaledale, Yorkshire.*
AUTUMN PALETTE — *Strathtummel, Perthshire.*
KEEP US SAFE — *Cloch Lighthouse, Gourock.*
A CHILD IS BORN — *Altar, Italian Chapel, Orkney.*

ACKNOWLEDGMENTS: **Ivan J. Belcher;** Beauty Spot. **James D. Cameron;** Highland Winter, Time And Tide, Autumn Palette. **Paul Felix;** Birds Of A Feather, Cotswold Corner. **V. K. Guy;** Going Fishing. **T. G. Hopewell;** Keep Us Safe. **Doug Houghton;** Firm Footing. **Douglas Laidlaw;** Inspiration, The Music Maker, Under Cyprus Skies. **Duncan I. McEwan;** Welcome! **Oakleaf;** Cloudless Day. **Polly Pullar;** Sitting Comfortably. **Clifford Robinson;** Blue Horizon. **Phil Seale;** Frosty Frame, In Pastures Green, Capture The Moment, Nature's Decorations. **Roddy Simpson;** Reflections, A Child Is Born. **Willie Shand;** On The Right Track, Good News. **Sheila Taylor;** Coming Alive, Lost To The World. **SW Images;** Reach For The Sky. **Richard Watson;** Pure Perfection, The Great Outdoors, The Falls.

Printed and Published by D. C. Thomson & Co., Ltd.,
185 Fleet Street, London EC4A 2HS.
© D. C. Thomson & Co., Ltd., 2007